Shabbos Sparks

Sefer Bamidbar

Compiled by: Refoel Berel Chesler

הסכמה מאת הרב דניאל יעקב טראויש שליט״א

ב״ה

"*Chizkia* said in the name of Rebbi Yermiah in the name of Rebbi Shimon bar Yochai 'I have seen *bnei aliya* and they are few in number. If there are one thousand, myself and my son are included. If there are one hundred, myself and my son are included. If there are two, myself and my son are included'" (*Sukah* 45b).

Rebbi Shimon starts off by saying that he has seen *bnei aliya*. If so why does he afterwards suggest that it could be that the only two *bnei aliya* are himself and his son? Does this not contradict *Rebbi Shimon's* original assertion?

We can suggest that in truth only the *ben aliya* himself knows if he is really a *ben aliya*. Only he is familiar with the deep feelings of love and fear of Hashem that reside in his heart, the challenges and struggles that he has to deal with, and the myriad of other *nisyonos* that face a *ben aliya*. For this reason, only the person himself can testify if he is really a *ben aliya* or not.

Over the past years I have had the privilege to get to know R' Refoel Chesler. As a Rosh Kollel, I have met *bnei aliya* and I truly believe that R' Refoel can be included in this group. He has decided to print his excellent *Divrei Torah* for the *rabim*, and I give R' Refoel my heartfelt blessing he should have the greatest success in this and all other endeavors that he sets out to do.

B'ahava gedola,

Rabbi Daniel Yaakov Travis
Rosh Kollel Toras Chaim, Yerushalayim

הסכמה מאת הרב דוד נוסבוים שליט"א

ב"ה

Although I have not met R' Refoel in person, we have discussed on the phone many matters of Torah. I find his thirst for Torah knowledge to be inspiring and impressive. He sent me a few pages of his manuscript and he quotes from many reliable sources for his Divrei Torah including from his Rabeim which I find refreshing to see the kesher between the Rebbe and the Talmid clearly visible and appreciated. IY"H he should be successful in his desire to spread Torah and encourage others to spend more time learning the weekly parsha.

Dovid Nussbaum
R"M Yeshiva Toras Chaim/Denver

הסכמה מאת הרב אברהם לייב שיינבוים שליט״א

ב״ה

It has been my privilege and pleasure to have read Refoel Berel Chesler's [Shabbos Sparks] on a weekly basis. His selection of *divrei Torah* is well thought out, as well as his presentation. He is a true *Ben Torah* who seeks to glorify HaShem by disseminating His word. *Yasheir Kocho l'Oraysa*.

Rabbi A. Leib Scheinbaum

הסכמה מאת הרב יוסף סבג שליט״א

ב״ה

Rabbi Yosef Sebag
dafyomireview.com

I have looked over an excerpt of the "Shabbos Sparks" by Refoel Berel Chesler and it is full of beautiful *chidushim* on the *parsha*.

I have corresponded with the author over the years and he is a "new bottle full of old wine", with pure "fear of Heaven before his wisdom" which endures.

Refoel is a *ben aliyah* with strong desire to grow and help others grow. *Ken yirbu b'yisrael*!

May his writings be a source of *chizuk* and inspiration for those who read them and may the author ascend up the ladder of Torah and *yirah* to become one of the *Gedolei Hador*, be'H.

Yosef Sebag, Tamuz 2 5780

הסכמה מאת הרב הלל גולדברג שליט״א

ב״ה

An effective anthologist is an artist. R' Refoel Berel Chesler, who appreciates all of the color lines in the spectrum of Torah, has a keen instinct for just which source to turn to in order to illuminate a word, a verse, or a longer segment on this infinite spectrum. Sometimes his source is relatively contemporary and sometimes it is older or even ancient, so that in reading his work, one is introduced to the different approaches of many commentators in addition to a fresh reading of the immediate text at hand.

It is a pleasing experience to study R' Berel Refoel's work. It is not forced. It is not extraneous or focused on side points. It is well expressed.

To see in a young student of Torah such a broad approach that also hones in on important teachings is itself inspiring. Lo almein Yisrael.

May Hashem bless R' Refoel Berel's Torah study and give us the benefit of its fruits for years and decades to come. May those fruits continue to blossom and grow as R' Refoel Berel, im yirzeh Hashem, probes ever deeper into the layers of Torah.

Rabbi Hillel Goldberg
Author of Hallel HaKohen on Biur HaGra, Yoreh Deah 110 and 201.
Denver, Colorado

ב"ה

I enjoyed reading the excerpts of your sefer on Chumash. You brought together many interesting, enlightening, and inspiring thoughts from many great luminaries. Your love of Torah and sincerity shine through your sefer. I am sure that everyone will benefit from your sefer, and at the same time, find it enjoyable. May Hashem give you the privilege to spread the beautiful words of Torah Hakadoshah.

Yehoshua Kalish

הסכמה מאת הרב ישראל מאיר קגן שליט"א

ב"ה

[illegible]

הנה הרה"ג שליט"א עשה דבר
נאה ומתוקן אשר ליקט על כל המצוות הנוגעים לבר
דברים נאים ומעוררים מכמה ספרים וספרים
וגם מה שאמרו מרבותינו התלמידים זי"ע, והוסיף
עוד נופך מן דיליה עניינים יסודיים ומשלים
את הכל והוא מסודר יפה להבין גם מה
שאינו בלשונו.
ויהי שיתקבלו הדברים בפני רבנן.
הכותב לכבוד התורה ולומדיה
ישראל מאיר הכהן קגן
רמ

הסכמה מאת הרב שלום קלמר שליט״א

בס״ד

שלום וכל טוב

לכבוד הבחור רפאל עוזיאל נ״י

אחרי דרישת שלום כראוי, הנני לגבת
בשמח על רבית הספר שחיברו וכיני עד
ל' רבש בדרך פלא ועברו עמוקים
ומחזקים ונבגל מועד הספר, ובי רבון
שיבזב ויעיני הלכן עוזין לאקתא
רבה, בתורה ובראה, ויזכה על הכנסת
האורות כתורה.

ועיין בתחילה "עוד כאן מן הגיוונים
לכבוד התורה,

שלום קלמר

בס"ד

ACKNOWLEDGEMENTS

Ribbono Shel Olam! 'Thank You' is not nearly sufficient to express my gratitude to You for enabling me to put together this *sefer* and publish it, and, further, while still a yeshiva bochur. Additionally, I am deeply grateful in a more general sense for all Your *chasadim* and Your constant Guiding Hand in my life. It is absolutely indescribable all the *berachos* and assistance You have given and shown me throughout my life so far -- and I myself don't even know anywhere near all of them! However, being that those are the closest, most appropriate words I can find within the limitation of my vocabulary, this is what I must say: Thank You! Your continuous *chasadim* in my life know no bounds, and, while I don't deserve any of it, my *tefillah* to You is, please continue to send me Your sweet *Siyata d'Shmaya* in everything.

A special thank you to my wonderful parents and siblings, and of course to all of my amazing Rebbeim. You have all helped me so much in innumerable and immeasurable ways, and I am indebted to all of you. There is so much more to say, but I hope you will forgive me for saying it short and sweet. I hope this *sefer* will bring you *nachas*.

I must express my gratitude to all of the Rabbonim who have made themselves available to me and have helped, encouraged, and advised me, sometimes even without knowing me personally. Your help is really appreciated.

Although I am attempting to be brief, I must single out and thank my friend, Netanel Schachter, as it was he who inspired me to begin writing. Thank you.

And finally, thank you to HebrewBooks.org, who helped make certain *seforim* available to me, even when I did not have access to them.

I ask that everyone should please be *mochel* me for not thanking them all individually as they deserve to be, however, as noted, I am trying to be brief, but know that you and what you do are appreciated.

***

INTRODUCTORY REMARKS

'Shabbos Sparks' is a name that I feel (mostly) fits the intention of this *sefer*. Why only mostly? Because it is my hope that the perusal of it will not be limited to *Shabbosos* alone. Besides that point, though, it is meant to convey the warmth and glow of Shabbos, together with the fire of Torah, illuminating and burning through many sparks (see *Yirmiyahu* 23:29; *Shabbos* 88b; *Sanhedrin* 34a). It is my sincere hope that the reader/learner of this *sefer* will feel both as they go through the *divrei Torah* and *vortlach* within. Most of them lean towards the more *hashkafic* and *mussar* side of things, with practical and hopefully inspiring lessons. To that end, it is my fervent wish that aside from being used to find *vortlach* on the *Parsha*, the messages within the *divrei Torah* and stories should be taken to heart and perhaps implemented in everyday life.

The format of the *sefer* is to bring a handful of insights and *vortlach* on the *Parsha*, with a couple stories (of varying lengths) at the end, which can be tied in to a *passuk* in the *Parsha*. In a play on words, I entitled that section 'Maasim Tovim.' It is a *likut sefer*, meaning that most of the material has been gleaned and adapted from the teachings of our *Gedolim*, whom I quote by name within the piece, and you will most often find the source in the back of the *sefer*. Uncredited *vortlach* are little insights which Hashem has granted the compiler.

And finally, while I have tried to eliminate and correct all errors, as a human being, it is inevitable that some will be found, and I beg the pardon of the reader, as well as ask that if you should encounter any, please let me know at aishkodesh611@gmail.com.

Table of Contents

פרשת במדבר

Parshas Bamidbar

וידבר השם אל משה במדבר סיני
'And Hashem spoke to Moshe in the Wilderness of
Sinai'
(Bamidbar 1:1)

Teaches the *Midrash* (*Bamidbar Rabbah* 1:7): With three things the Torah was given: With fire, with water, and in the wilderness. And why was it given with these three things? To tell to us that just like these things are free to everyone, so too the Torah is free to everyone [and all who want can come and learn it for no charge at all].[1]

❀❀❀❀❀❀❀❀❀❀❀❀❀❀

---

[1] Furthermore, we actually get paid great reward for learning it!

ויִדַבֵּר הַשֵׁם אֶל מֹשֶׁה בְּמִדְבַּר סִינַי
'And Hashem spoke to Moshe in the Wilderness of Sinai'
(Bamidbar 1:1)

Says HaRav Shimshon Dovid Pincus *zt"l*: As is known, the Revelation at *Har Sinai*, and the Giving of the Torah were in the wilderness. And some ask; why wasn't the Torah given in *Eretz Yisroel*? Afterall, we know from the *Gemara* (**Bava Basra** 158b) that the very air of the Land makes one wiser, and its holiness would have had influence on the Jewish People. Plus, a lot of *Mitzvos* in the Torah are actually only able to be kept in Israel. So why, indeed, did Hashem give us the Torah before we reached *Eretz Yisroel*?

The explanation, says Rav Pincus, seems to comes from the exposition of **Chazal** (*Mishnah Taanis* 4:8) on the verse in *Shir HaShirim* (3:12), '*On the day of His[2] wedding, and on the day of the joy of His heart*', that this 'wedding' refers to *Matan Torah*. The connection and attachment of *Klal Yisroel* with HaKadosh Baruch Hu is through the Torah.

In order for this connection to be complete, without a diversion of attention to other things, the Torah needed to be something that was the only thing between them. Now, if the Jews had already entered *Eretz Yisroel*

---

[2] According to one interpretation, '*His*' refers to Hashem, and according to another it doesn't. See the *Meforshim* there.

before *Matan Torah*, it was liable to happen that everyone would turn to their farming, produce, and the like, and what would be with the Torah?

The 40 years in the wilderness without any involvement in the field or vineyard strengthened our connection to Hashem. They were like the *Yichud* room at a wedding -- just between the husband and wife. We've never heard of people making their wedding in their house, because if they did, then things in the kitchen might need tending to, etc., and that is not the time for such things!

In the wilderness, since it wasn't yet applicable to perform certain *Mitzvos* which can only be done in Israel, we were engaged primarily in the Torah, which set firmly the special connection of *Klal Yisroel* to Hashem.א

וידבר השם אל משה. . .
'And Hashem spoke to Moshe. . .'
(Bamidbar 1:1)

There are seventy letters in the first verse of *Parshas Bamidbar*. This alludes to the countings in this *Parsha*, for the *Bnei Yisroel* had come down to Egypt with only seventy souls, and now -- of just males from 20-60 years old -- there were 603,550! (See **Ramban** *zt"l* to v. 45).

16

וידבר השם אל משה ... שאו את ראש

***'And Hashem spoke to Moshe. . . "Take a count [lit.
'Lift the head']'"***

(Bamidbar 1:1-2)

R ashi *zt"l* brings that because of how precious *Bnei Yisroel* are to Hashem, He counts us very often, as we see in different places in the Torah.

HaRav Yerucham Levovitz *zt"l* gives us a little perspective on this: It is the nature of a person who acquires money and loves it, to touch it, and count it, and count it again, and again. And really, what is the purpose of all these countings? The person already knows from their first tally how much money they have! But because of how much they love their money, they keep going back and counting it, because they desire it, and they are so often thinking about it.

This is the thing that *Rashi* teaches us here: There wouldn't seem to be a need for this particular counting, but because of how precious we are to Hashem, and He loves us and desires in us, He counts us very often -- for He is always thinking of us.[ב]

**וידבר השם אל משה... באחד לחדש השני בשנה
השנית לצאתם מארץ מצרים לאמר: שאו את ראש**

***'And Hashem spoke. . . in the second year to their
going out from the land of Egypt, saying: "Take a
count [lit. 'Lift the head]"'***

(Bamidbar 1:1-2)

איש על דגלו באתת לבית אבתם יחנו בני ישראל
*'Each man by his banner,[3] with the signs of their
fathers' house shall the Children of Israel encamp'*
(Bamidbar 2:2)

Why, asks **HaRav Yaakov Kaminetzky** *zt"l*, was a full year waited from the *Yetzias Mitzraim* until the establishment of the banners?

In truth, he answers beautifully, the banners were something that could have caused discord, because they each had different colors, and unique insignias on them, and the banner of each of the Tribes had a different picture on it, which emphasized that each Tribe had its own distinct and separate traits and qualities.

But once there was one central, uniting, point for all of them, i.e., the *Mishkan*, and they were all encamping around it, then the banners would not cause any separateness, and everyone would stand at their unique charge, with no lack of unity.

It's like a person, says Rav Yaakov: Just because one's ears were created to hear, and the eyes to see, would you even entertain the thought that there would be disunity or strife between them?! So too, with a nation; once everyone was

---

[3] Please note that according to a different translation, many of the times we use the word banner, it is 'division'.

centered around one focal-point, then there would be no worry about any lack of unity.

And therefore, all the while that the *Mishkan* had not yet been erected, and thus there was no center of spirituality, the entire Jewish People was kept as one unit with one banner for everyone. But <u>after</u> the *Mishkan* was erected, there was no longer a worry about any harm coming from having different banners, and therefore it was only now -- a month after the erection of the *Mishkan* -- that the banners were dealt with.[1]

Similarly, my *Rebbe*, **HaRav Avraham Kaplan** *shlit"a* said on the banners that they represent the concept that we all have our individual, unique gifts and talents – yes, every single person. And nobody else possesses your exact capabilities. We needn't be jealous of others' blessings, for we all have the unique ones that are meant exclusively for us.

לשמעון שלמיא-ל בן צוריש-די
'To Shimon; Shelumiel son of TzuriShaddai.'
(Bamidbar 1:6)

In the *Midrash Tanchuma* on *Parshas Pinchas* it is taught that Shelumiel was called three names: Shelumiel ben TzuriShaddai, Shaul ben HaCanaanis, and Zimri ben

Salu. And what was his real name? Shelumiel ben TzuriShaddai.

These other names, says **HaRav Zalman Sorotzkin** *zt"l*, were seemingly nicknames given in accordance with his deeds (see *Tanchuma Pinchas* 2). However, he brings from the **Maharzu** *zt"l* something that seems to imply that his name was really Shaul ben HaCanaanis -- that he was the namesake of the one who was among those going down to Egypt. (See Bereishis 46:10). So, then the question is, what <u>was</u> his name?

Elucidates Rav Sorotzkin; what appears to be the explanation is that his name was actually Shelumiel ben TzuriShaddai, and when he was a righteous person he was called by this name. But when he began to turn away from the Way of Hashem, his and his father's names didn't seem good to him anymore, so he changed them to names which can be interpreted to have very negative connotations. And since he changed his name, he changed to a different man, as it were, and he was caught by his *yetzer hara* and became a sinner who also caused others to sin, until they nicknamed him Zimri ben Salu, which alludes to his terrible sin with the daughters of Moav and Midyan (see *Tanchuma* ibid.).

And from this we learn, says Rav Sorotzkin *zt"l*; that a Jew who changes his name and his father's name to non-Jewish names, paves the road for himself to go in the ways of the gentiles, and is liable to sin and cause the masses to sin.[7]

❊ ❊ ❊ ❊ ❊ ❊ ❊ ❊ ❊ ❊ ❊ ❊ ❊ ❊ ❊

ונסע אהל מועד מחנה הלוים בתוך המחנת
'And the Tent of Meeting, the camp of the Leviim, shall travel in the midst of the camps'
(Bamidbar 2:17)

Says the **Chofetz Chaim** *zt"l*: Since the Torah rested in the *Aron* (Ark), which was in the Tent of Meeting, the Tent of Meeting needed to always be *'in the midst'* of the camps; in the middle -- no closer to one and no farther from another. Just like the *Bimah* is [in a lot of *Shuls*] in the middle of the *Shul*, and like the Tree of Life was *'in the midst'* of *Gan Eden*, as the **Targum Onkelos** translates it, *'in the <u>middle</u> of the Garden.'*

So too, the Torah is the 'Tree of Life', and everyone needs to center around it with it in the middle.ח

This lesson is so very important to internalize: To make the Torah the centerpiece of our lives -- what everything revolves around. And as we come into the Festival of Receiving the Torah, Shavuos, we must try to re-accept the Torah *b'Shleimus* (with completeness), and rededicate ourselves to this amazing gift, and the Giver of it.

❊ ❊ ❊ ❊ ❊ ❊ ❊ ❊ ❊ ❊ ❊ ❊ ❊ ❊ ❊

Parshas *Bamidbar* is almost always read the Shabbos before Shavuos. And in the rare occurrence that it isn't, it still is quite close. **Tosafos**, in fact, in *Gemara Megillah* 31b say that it was indeed arranged that *Parshas*

Bamidbar be read before Shavuos. *Tosafos* gives a reason for this (see there), but explains **HaRav Moshe Feinstein** *zt"l* that there is really a great connection between *Parshas Bamidbar* and Shavuos. And that is in the following way:

Unfortunately, some people are lax in the study of Torah because they think that they can't reach any kind of high level in it.

However, the counting of the Jewish People combats this feeling. For, as we know, when Hashem commands Moshe Rabbeinu to take a census of the People, the wording used literally means to lift up. שאו. This is because it uplifts everyone when they see that in the count, they are equal to a great person, in that a *Gadol* isn't counted as more than one, and they aren't counted as less than one. They both count as one. And if this is the case, then they too are able to reach a high level, just like the *Gedolim*!

And therefore, concludes Rav Moshe beautifully, before Shavuos, we need to read *Parshas Bamidbar*, the *Parsha* of the countings, which teaches us that in this way -- when we realize that we, too, have the capability to rise to great heights in Torah -- we are able to accept the Torah and learn it.[1]

❀❀❀❀❀❀❀❀❀❀❀❀❀❀❀

❧*Maasim Tovim*☙

במדבר סיני
'In the Wilderness of Sinai'
(Bamidbar 1:1)

My first encounter with **HaRav Yehoshua Kalish** *shlit"*a came when I was visiting a friend of mine in Far Rockaway. We were going to *Yeshivas Derech Eisan*, also known plainly as Yeshiva of Far Rockaway, and I was going to see what I thought of it for my *Beis Midrash* years. We mounted the stone steps which lead up to the building, and as I reached the top, I noticed a *Rav* with a white beard who I thought I recognized, speaking with some *bochurim*. "Are you Rav Kalish?" I asked him. He turned to me, and, in the incredible humility that is so characteristic of him -- as I learned from the many later conversations that I have been *zoche* to have with him after this initial meeting -- he replied, "I'm not Rabbi Kalish. That's Rabbi Kalish," and pointed to his son. "I'm fake." he said with a smile.

My *Rebbe*, **HaRav Daniel Yaakov Travis** *shlit"a* told me that Rav Kalish learns the entire *Shas* every year, and from speaking to him, one can easily see that he is an outstanding Torah scholar. But despite this -- or perhaps, in large part <u>because</u> of this -- he is incredibly humble. True Torah study and humility go together.

במדבר סיני
'In the Wilderness of Sinai'

(Bamidbar 1:1)

M*ori v'Rebbe*, **HaRav Elyakim Rosenblatt** *zt"l* also embodied humility -- in so many different ways, which manifested themselves throughout his long life and many interactions. An example of this is that I once told him that his written *shiurim* were really great. Even though he obviously put so much effort and toil into them, his reply was simply *"Baruch Hashem."* No credit for himself -- just thanks to Hashem.

❧❦

שאו את ראש כל עדת בני ישראל
'Take a count of the entire assembly of the Children of Israel'
(Bamidbar 1:2)

My *Rebbe*, the *mashgiach*, **HaRav Mordechai Finkelman** *shlit"a* related during one of his *mussar shmuessen* that he was once at a hotel for a convention for *Rabbanim*, and he saw a very elderly man sitting in the audience. Wanting to show respect for a *zakein* (elder), Rav Finkelman went over to him and spoke with him. The man told him that he was a *Bobover chossid*, and he had survived the Holocaust, and he told the following story:

In the Ghetto which he was in, there were 1,000 Jews, and one day, the wicked Nazis *yemach shemam* gathered 100 of them and told them that a brick of butter had been stolen, and they were looking for the "culprit." If the "thief" would come forward and confess, then they would all be okay, but if not, all 100 of them would be shot.

Now, there were two *bochurim* who were brothers which he knew, by the name of Buxbaum. One of them, Naftali Buxbaum, came forward and confessed to having stolen the butter -- even though, of course, he had nothing to do with it, but was trying to save 99 lives, as he knew that nobody else would have the courage to admit it, even if they had taken it. He claimed that he had stolen the butter to feed his brother.

Having found the "culprit", a Kapo came and led Naftali somewhere, where he was to be shot. The Kapo asked -- or more yelled at him -- the question "What did you do?" to which he replied that he stole a stick of butter. Why did he do it, questioned the Kapo. "To feed my brother," Naftali replied. "And are you afraid?" the wicked Kapo prodded. "No." Naftali answered calmly. The Kapo yelled his question again, and when this young *bochur* gave the same calm reply, he asked him why he wasn't scared. "Because," Naftali explained, "I know that I am a golden person; I have lived a golden life, and when I die, I will go to a golden place. You, however, are a dark person. You have lived a dark life, and when you die, you will go to a dark place -- and I should be afraid?"

This calm, deep reply infuriated the Kapo, and miraculously, he said that to waste a German bullet on him wasn't worth it, and *Baruch Hashem*, Naftali's life was spared! As the **Chovos HaLevavos** (*Shaar HaBitochon*) speaks about, when one truly trusts in Hashem, they will remain calm no matter the circumstances!

פרשת נשא

Parshas Nasso

וידבר השם אל משה לאמר : נשא את ראש בני גרשון
*'And Hashem spoke to Moshe, saying: "Take a count
[lit. 'lift up the head'] of the sons of Gershon. . .'"*
(Bamidbar 4:21-22)

Why, it is asked, was the work of the families of Gershon, the firstborn of the sons of Levi, spoken of <u>after</u> that of the families of Kehas, which was discussed at the end of last *Parsha*? The *Midrash*[4] explains that since the families of Kehas carried the *Aron*, inside of which was the Torah, they preceded the families of Gershon.

However, asks the **Kli Yakar** a very fundamental question: Why was the duty of carrying the *Aron* not given to the families of Gershon, to honor him, in accordance with his status as firstborn?

He suggests that HaKadosh Baruch Hu wanted to show that *'the wise will inherit honor'*[5], in order to teach people that they should honor those who study Torah, just like Kehas was discussed first because the *Bnei Kehas* carried

---

[4] *Bamidbar Rabbah* 6:1

[5] *Mishlei* 3:35

the *Aron*, which had in it the Word of Hashem. But if He had given the *Aron* to the families of Gershon to carry, people would say that it was because he was the firstborn that he was counted first, and it was not because of the importance of the job of carrying the *Aron*. Therefore, the carrying of the *Aron* was passed to the families of Kehas, and he was counted first, and through this, everyone would know to give honor and respect to Torah, and to those who learn it.

Adds **HaRav Avraham Leib Scheinbaum** *shlit"a*: We wonder if this is the proper way. Is it appropriate to arrogate the function of carrying the *Aron* for the ones who, by virtue of their sequence in birth, should have been accorded this privilege, just to prove a point -- that carrying the *Aron* was a holy and privileged endeavor, worthy of distinction?

HaRav Baruch Mordechai Ezrachi *shlit"a* derives a powerful lesson from here. For *Bnei Gershon* to be counted second, so that *Bnei Kehas* who carried the *Aron* could precede them, is in itself an honor for *Bnei Gershon*. They were being distinguished by being counted <u>second,</u> since being second means that <u>they</u> were giving honor to the *Aron*. In other words, *Bnei Gershon* did not lose distinction by being counted second. In fact, they benefited because their status was raised as a result of what they had relinquished! This act of abdication elevated them and made them a *nesui rosh* (lifted head).

This is the meaning of *naso*, to "elevate/count, *Bnei Gershon*." This elevation came as a result of their being counted second, thereby demonstrating that they were giving honor to the *Aron HaKodesh*. Ironically, being in the background was what brought them to the foreground.א

In a similar vein, **HaRav Chaim Kanievsky** *shlit"a* wonders why this *Parsha* begins with the discussion about the *Bnei Gershon*, and it wasn't put at the end of last *Parsha* with the topic of the *Bnei Kehas*.

And he explains that, as we know, Gershon was the firstborn. But Kehas was *zocheh* (merited) to have Moshe and Aharon come from him, and therefore the *Bnei Kehas* were the bearers of the *Aron*, and went before *Bnei Gershon* in the discussions of their service.

Yet Gershon didn't sin that he should be taken down from his special position -- therefore, for his honor, he was given the special privilege that a *Parsha* begin by speaking about him.ב

ואיש את קדשיו לו יהיו איש אשר יתן לכהן לו יהיה
'And a man, his holy things shall be his; a man, what he gives to the Kohen shall be his.'
(Bamidbar 5:10)

Says the **Chofetz Chaim** *zt"l*: We can read these words very literally. Although, sometimes, the *yetzer hara* tries to make fleeting material pursuits seem enduring, and like they are what will help you, in truth, they don't stay with you, and they don't help you! What are the only things that really and truly belong to a person, and will stay with them forever? The *passuk* tells us -- our "holy things." Meaning, whatever Torah and *Mitzvos* we accumulate, they will remain with us forever. Both in this World and the Next. And furthermore, "what we give to the *Kohen*," i.e. the funds, resources, etc. we give and allocate for others, they too will remain with us eternally. These things are truly ours.[1]

❀ ❀ ❀ ❀ ❀ ❀ ❀ ❀ ❀ ❀ ❀ ❀ ❀ ❀

Bamidbar 5:11-31: The *Sotah*:[6]

The Torah speaks about a woman who was suspected by her husband of potential infidelity, and he warned her not to go into seclusion with a certain man, but she violated the warning, and was in private with that man for at least a small amount of time. She is suspected of having committed adultery, and we don't know whether she did or didn't. If she doesn't confess to having sinned, the Torah prescribes a procedure through which she is tested.

The woman is brought to the *Mishkan* or *Beis HaMikdash*, and the *Kohen* puts together a special potion-like

---

[6] For a more in-depth discussion and further details on this topic, see *Chumash* commentaries to this portion, and **Gemara Sotah.**

mixture. He takes water from the *Kiyor*[7], and puts in earth from the ground of the *Mishkan,* or from underneath the stone floor of the *Beis HaMikdash.*[8] He adjures the woman with certain oaths (see v. 19-22), and he writes down the oaths, which include in them the Name of Hashem, on a scroll, and erases the writing -- yes, with the Name -- into the waters! Even though it is virtually always forbidden to erase Hashem's Name, in this specific case, this is what the Torah mandates. The suspected wife drinks these waters, and if she was guilty, then she dies. But if she was truly innocent, she emerges unscathed, and in fact receives a big blessing.

Explains **HaRav Yaakov Kamenetzky** *zt"l*: The nature of a man is that if he begins to suspect his wife's fidelity, the doubt won't leave his heart unless HaKadosh Baruch Hu Himself assures him that she is innocent.

Even though in most cases in Torah-Law, we rely on the testimony of two witnesses, the husband still likely wouldn't believe them completely if they told him that his wife didn't do anything wrong. Their testimony wouldn't be good enough to quiet his feelings and suspicions.

Therefore, says Rav Yaakov, the Torah commands us to erase the scroll -- with the Name of Hashem -- into the waters, and have the woman drink them. This will be the test to know the truth. If the wife comes out unharmed, it is tantamount to the Testimony of Hashem Himself that

---

[7] **Rashi** from *Sifri.*
[8] *Sotah* 15b.

she is completely innocent of all suspicions. The "bitter" waters were an assurance that a wife who really didn't do anything wrong would be innocent even in her husband's eyes, without any doubt whatsoever.

And this is what the *Gemara*[9] means when it tells us that peace and harmony between husband and wife is so great, that the Torah says that the Name of Hashem would be erased in order to establish it!ᵀ

איש או אשה כי יפלא לנדר נדר נזיר להזיר להשם
'A man or woman who will separate themselves by taking a Nazirite vow to be a Nazir to Hashem.'
(Bamidbar 6:2)

From the juxtaposition of the section dealing with the *Sotah* and the one that discusses a *Nazir*, **Chazal** derive that if someone saw a *Sotah* in her degradation -- i.e. the humiliation she goes through during the procedure -- he should take a *Nazir* vow against having wine, (which symbolizes comestible desire).

My *Rebbe*, **HaRav Avraham Kaplan** *shlit"a* asks the question; this man saw the bad consequences of following one's desires firsthand -- so why should he take a vow of abstinence? Didn't he just get the message loud and clear?

---

9 *Chullin* 141a.

Answers my *Rebbe* beautifully; seeing or hearing a lesson is amazing. But it isn't enough. We must take a practical step forward, in the right direction, to really internalize it and take it to the next level.

❋ ❋ ❋ ❋ ❋ ❋ ❋ ❋ ❋ ❋ ❋ ❋ ❋ ❋

איש או אשה כי יפלא לנדר נדר נזיר להזיר להשם
'A man or woman who will separate themselves by taking a Nazirite vow to be a Nazir to Hashem.'
(Bamidbar 6:2)

Adapted from a *shmuess* of **HaRav Leib Chasman** *zt"l, Mori v'Rebbe*, **HaRav Elyakim Rosenblatt** *zt"l* expounds one of the messages of the *Nazir*: The Torah here speaks about the extraordinary greatness of the *Nazir*, who refrains from cutting his hair and drinking wine for thirty days. The Torah lauds and exalts him with praise upon praise. *'He is holy. . .'*;[10] he is not permitted to become *tamei* (ritually impure) even to bury his immediate family,[11] just as the law states concerning a *Kohen Gadol*. The Torah even proclaims that the very crown of Hashem lies upon the *Nazir*'s head.[12] Furthermore, the **Baal HaTurim** provides us with additional insight into the holiness and purity of the *Nazir*. He explains why the *Nazir* is not permitted to become *tamei* even for his immediate family. For if the Presence of Hashem would rest upon him due to his holy level of *Nezirus*, it should

---

[10] Bamidbar 6:8

[11] 6:7

[12] Ibid.

not be said that he is seeking assistance from the dead. People should not think that a *Nazir*, upon whom the *Shechina* (Divine Presence) could possibly rest, is beseeching the dead with prayers.

The big question is; what did the *Nazir* do to deserve all of this greatness? Doesn't Hashem usually reward each person according to his efforts? What extensive efforts did the *Nazir* do by merely refraining from cutting his hair and drinking wine for thirty days? Surely this required little effort, if any at all.

Furthermore, even if we were to say that the *Nazir* did exert much effort by refraining from cutting his hair and drinking wine, would he then be worthy of such extraordinarily disproportionate rewards? Would he be worthy of being proclaimed by the Torah as holy, of being equated to the *Kohen Gadol*, and of being possibly on par with a prophet of Hashem? Should he be worthy of wearing the crown of Hashem on his head? Are not these incredible rewards way out of proportion to his efforts?

Perhaps, according to the **Ibn Ezra** *zt"l*'s understanding of the meaning of *Nezirus*, these questions can be resolved. The Torah states, 'איש כי יפלא',[13] which the *Ibn Ezra* interprets to mean that the *Nazir* is doing something פלא, incredible. It is incredible because "most people of the world are in passionate pursuit of obtaining more and more temptations," while the *Nazir*, differentiating himself from the bulk of the population, is desperately

---

[13] Bamidbar 6:2

trying to break free and to disassociate himself from these temptations. He sees that his life consists of nothing more than amassing more and more material gain and experiencing more and more physical pleasures, with little or no deeper thought whatsoever as to why he was created and what his duties are on earth, and what is expected of him. He consequently comes to the realization that he must stop this downward spiral, and infuse himself with spirituality. He, thus, accepts upon himself the Nazirite vow to refrain from drinking wine and cutting his hair, in order to detach and break free from his meaningless pursuit of material and physical pleasures.

In light of the *Ibn Ezra*'s insight, our questions can now be answered. The greatness of the *Nazir* lies not merely from the fact that he abstains from cutting his hair and drinking wine for thirty days. Rather, the greatness of the *Nazir* lies in his purpose and intent in refraining from involvement in these activities. He is embarking upon a bold and courageous mission. He has taken upon himself to go out to battle against man's arch-enemy, the *yetzer hara* itself, head-on. What an extremely difficult path he has chosen! Not many people have the strength or the courage to be warriors setting out to "conquer their passions." The *Nazir* is the one with that innate greatness who strives to go against the trend of the masses, which is to indulge in all sorts of enticements and temptations. He goes "against his grain" of yearning for physical pleasures, and instead, he aspires to conquer his passions. The magnificent reward that the Torah bestows upon the *Nazir* is in direct proportion to the monumental effort that the *Nazir* puts forth in his fierce battle against the *yetzer hara*.

Although we are not suggesting actual *Nezirus*, concludes *Rabbeinu zt"l*, nevertheless the concept and ideals of *Nezirus* are something that we certainly should aspire to achieve. Every *Yiddishe Neshama* has that inherent potential within himself to attain the lofty spiritual level of the holy *Nazir*. The way to attain this heightened level of spirituality is to actively and aggressively go out to battle the adversary within us, the *yetzer hara*.

❀ ❀ ❀ ❀ ❀ ❀ ❀ ❀ ❀ ❀ ❀ ❀ ❀ ❀

קדש יהיה
'Holy he shall be'
(Bamidbar 6:5)

The *Gemara* derives from this that a regular term of *Nezirus* is 30 days, because the word "יהיה" (*'he shall be'*) has the numerical value of 30.

From this we can see, says the **Chofetz Chaim *zt"l***, how great is the strength of the Torah; for, from even one numerical value that is in the Written Torah, the Sages derived many pages-worth in *Maseches Nazir*.ח

❀ ❀ ❀ ❀ ❀ ❀ ❀ ❀ ❀ ❀ ❀ ❀ ❀

ויהי ביום כלות משה להקים את המשכן

'And it was on the day that Moshe finished erecting the Mishkan'
(Bamidbar 7:1)

Says **Rashi** *zt"l* from **Chazal**: The word כלות, 'finished' is written as if it were to be read כלת. This teaches us that on the day of the erection of the *Mishkan*, the Jews were like a bride, כלה, going to the *chuppah* (marriage canopy).

Explains **HaRav Elazar Menachem Mann Shach** *zt"l*; it's true -- on this day Moshe Rabbeinu completed the process of the *Mishkan*. But for the Jews, it was not an end nor completion, rather specifically now it was the <u>beginning</u> of new life. And this is the comparison to a bride entering to the *chuppah* -- because the *chuppah* for her is more the beginning of new life than it is the end of her days of youth. This, says Rav Shach, is a great principle in Torah: There is no 'finish', so to speak; everything is a corridor leading to another level of continuous ascent.[1]

ויאמר השם אל משה נשיא אחד ליום נשיא אחד ליום
יקריבו את קרבנם לחנכת המזבח
'And Hashem said to Moshe; "One prince for a day; one prince for a day, shall they bring their offering for the Dedication of the Altar."'
(Bamidbar 7:11)

After this introductory phrase, the Torah goes on to list which Prince of the Jewish People brought his offering on which day, and it goes into detail of what they each brought. The *Midrash* famously notes that, if you look, all of the offerings which the Princes brought were the same! In every detail! So, then the question is asked; what was the reason the Torah has to go into detail with the offering for each Prince, when they were all the same? Could it not have just said that they all brought such-and-such?

But we see a huge lesson from the fact that it is listed this way: It is easy to think, during *Minyan*, for example, when so many other people are *Davening*, does Hashem really care about my individual prayer? Does it really matter? I'm saying the same prayers as everyone else! And similar things in other circumstances.

Comes along the Torah, though, and it teaches us that Hashem <u>never</u> gets "tired" of our *Mitzvos*. The entire Jewish Nation could be doing the same *Mitzvah* at the same time and in the same way, and Hashem would love <u>your</u> *Mitzvah* just as much as if you were the only person in the world doing it.

And this doesn't just go for our *Mitzvos*; it also goes for us as a human being. There are so many people out there, but Hashem cares about and loves <u>each one</u> of us.

זאת חנכת המזבח ביום המשח אתו

'This was the dedication of the Altar on the day it was anointed'
(Bamidbar 7:84)

זאת חנכת המזבח אחרי המשח אתו
'This was the dedication of the Altar after it was anointed'
(Bamidbar 7:88)

Says Rebbe Avraham Mordechai Alter *zt"l*, the fourth *Gerrer Rebbe*: We must try to make sure that the *hischadshus*, the feeling of excitement and fervor when something is new, that awakens on the "day of the dedication" should stay with us afterwards and not become old. The dedication *'on the day it was anointed'* should stay also *'after it was anointed'*.[1]

❈ ❈ ❈ ❈ ❈ ❈ ❈ ❈ ❈ ❈ ❈ ❈ ❈

Parshas Nasso is the longest of all the *Parshiyos* in the Torah, and it has 176 verses. It has been noted that Chapter 119, the longest in *Tehillim*, also has 176 verses. And not only this, but the longest *Masechta*, **Bava Basra**, has 176 *dappim* (pages)! What is the significance of the number 176?

Perhaps we can suggest that if we look, 176 is the *Gematria* (numerical value) of the word **לעולם**, 'forever.' This alludes to us that the Torah we learn, the *Tehillim* we say, and the like -- those things last forever. It is not the material things we amass, but rather the good things that we perform.[14]

☙*Maasim Tovim*❧

איש או אשה כי יעשו מכל חטאת האדם . . . והתודו
את חטאתם אשר עשו והשיב

'A man or woman who will do from any of the sins of
a person. . . And they shall confess their sin that they
did, and they shall return. . .'
(Bamidbar 5:6-7)

Here, the Torah goes back to speaking about the sin of theft. . .
(Rashi zt"l *from* **Sifri)**

There was once a nice woman who had been blessed with lots of money in gold coins and nuggets. Afraid that someone might, *Chas v'Shalom*, steal the gold, she had to find a good place to hide them where nobody would suspect, just in case anyone ever broke in, or the like.

In her house, she had several ceramic jars of honey, and she realized that due to the similarity in color to the gold, besides for being a place where nobody would suspect, this was a perfect place to hide the gold! So, she divided up her gold pieces and put them at the bottom of the

---

[14] See above, on 5:10.

honey jars. They blended in perfectly! Still, every so often, she would take a ladle, and scoop to the bottom of the jars, just to make sure that the coins were still there, and nothing had happened.

One time, she had to travel somewhere, and of course she couldn't take her jars of honey with her, so she asked one of her neighbors -- a man she trusted -- if he could look after her jars of honey while she was away. This was a very small request, and the man kindly agreed.

The man was true to his word. He kept the jars of honey with him in his home, and made sure they didn't get broken, damaged, or used. But one day, he was making a certain recipe, which called for honey, and he didn't have any in his house. It would be such a bother to have to go out to the market and purchase honey, and here he had several jars of this nice honey sitting in his house. Surely the woman wouldn't mind if he just took a tiny bit for his recipe -- after all, before she got back, he would buy some, and refill what he had taken.

He undid the lid of one of the honey jars, and dipped a ladle deeply in. But when he drew it back up, he found a surprise in it! A golden nugget! He dipped the ladle in again, and came up with some more! Now it all made sense -- why this woman was so specific about having her jars of mere honey safeguarded. There was something much more valuable inside, indeed! Although he was a trustworthy and honest person, he gave in to the pull of his *yetzer hara*, and emptied out all the jars, removed the golden pieces from them, and then replaced the honey back in, and closed them up.

When the woman returned from her trip, she went quickly to his home to take back her jars of honey. The man graciously gave them all back, and she left to her own house. Once inside the privacy of her own home, she opened up one of the jars, and nervously dipped her ladle inside to make sure that the gold was still there. But when she pulled back up the ladle, it had only honey in it! Becoming more frightened by the moment, she opened up and checked all her other jars, but they too, were empty of everything but honey. She was devastated. Quickly, though, regaining her wits, she realized that her neighbor must have taken the gold. So, she went to him, asking him pointed questions, but he denied even knowing that there had been one bit of gold in the jars, much less taking it!

But who else could have taken it? It must have been this man! In her desperation, she went to the palace of Shaul HaMelech to present her case before him and hoped that he would see the truth of the matter. Once given entry before the king, she poured out her case and claim before him. He asked if she had any witnesses that could verify that she had gold in those jars in the first place, but of course she had none! Without witnesses or proof, the verdict was clear: No action could be taken.

The woman left the palace crying hysterically. All her wealth had seemingly been hopelessly taken away from her. At that time, Dovid HaMelech -- who wasn't a king yet -- was only an adolescent or teenager, and as he was walking along, he heard this woman sobbing. He went over and asked what the problem was, and she unburdened her sad tale onto him.

Dovid was very upset at this woman's plight, and he really believed that she was telling the truth. But how could he prove it? Suddenly, a brilliant idea struck him! He asked the woman to bring him all her honey pots, which she did, and he emptied them out and then brought them before Shaul HaMelech. To the astonishment of everyone present, though, he began to break apart all the jars! "What's he doing?" the question flew around. But Dovid knew what he was doing.

After smashing the ceramic jars, he started to pick among the shards, until he found, stuck to the inside of one of them, a piece of gold! And then he found another one on another shard, until several had been gathered together! Being that honey is extremely sticky, he knew that some gold would have stuck to the inside of the jars.

This was clear proof of the woman's claim, and, being that the accusation fell on the man whom she had entrusted them with, he was called before the king and accused of the theft. He broke down and confessed to his great sin, and he promptly returned the money to the good woman.ח

והתודו את חטאתם אשר עשו והשיב

'And they shall confess their sin that they did, and they shall return. . .'
(Bamidbar 5:7)

The **Baal Shem of Michelstadt** *zt"l*[15] once told a certain person that he was supposed to go around telling stories about him. Although it might have seemed like a strange request, the man complied with his *Rebbe's* instructions.

Once, this man heard that there was a certain person who would pay someone for every story about the *Baal Shem*. He went to this man's town, and came to his house for Shabbos, and the man was going to pay him for literally every story.

Friday night came, and he was expected to tell some stories. But as he was going to relate one, he found that he couldn't remember any! His mind was a blank! This was quite disgruntling, but it wasn't such a big deal, because there was always tomorrow. But all throughout Shabbos, he just couldn't recall any stories!

Shabbos departed, and the next morning, he was ready to leave the man's house -- both of them disappointed. But as he was just going, a story came to him! So he rushed to go tell his host, who was quite excited to hear.

---

[15] Please note that this story is often told in the name of the **Baal Shem Tov** *zt"l*.

He began: Once, the *Baal Shem* had gone with his *talmidim* (or *Chassidim*) on a trip, and they came to a heavily non-Jewish town, and stopped there. None of the *talmidim* knew why, though. Now, it happened that it was the day of the gentile holiday that falls out around Pesach, and the priest of the town was giving a sermon to a mass of townspeople in the town square. On such days, anti-Semitic violence was especially kindled.

The *Baal Shem* gave one of the *talmidim* very surprising instructions: He was to go through the crowds of people, and all the way up to the priest, and tell him to come to the *Baal Shem*. The *talmid* was understandably quite frightened to do this. He was clearly Jewish, and who knew what would happen to him, walking through a crowd of non-Jews being aroused to anti-Semitism! But he had to obey his *Rebbe*.

The *talmid* made his way to the town square, and then through the thick crowds, until he reached the dais on which the priest was delivering his speech. Astonishingly, nobody seemed to even take notice of him! Now for the next part, though: "The *Baal Shem* wants to see you." he said to the priest. The priest actually got a little flustered at the mention of the name, but he told the *talmid* that he couldn't come now.

So, the *talmid* made his way through the crowds and town, back to the *Baal Shem* and reported what had happened. Again, nobody seemed to even notice him. When the *Baal Shem* heard the priest's negative response, he told the *talmid* to go back, and this time, to tell him that he needed to come now, or it would be too late.

So, apprehensively, the *talmid* walked back again to the town square, through the crowds, and up to the dais. Still, it seemed as though not a single person saw him. "The *Baal Shem* said that you must come now, or it will be too late." He said to the priest. The priest now looked very scared, and gave in. He made an excuse to the townspeople of why he had to go, and made his way to the *Baal Shem*, together with the *talmid*. At that point, the priest entered a room alone with the *Baal Shem*, and stayed there for some time. Nobody knew what happened or what was said during that meeting, but he left crying. The *talmidim* realized that this "priest" must have been a lost Jewish Soul until then, but nobody knew what became of him afterwards.

As the storyteller finished his tale, it was now his host's turn to tell him something. He revealed that he was that priest! As a young man, he had left *frumkeit* and eventually, he had blended in to the non-Jews almost completely, and ended up becoming a priest. The *Baal Shem* had come to the town to bring him back. And when he entered the room together with the *Baal* Shem, he was finally going to do *teshuva*. He asked the *Baal Shem*, though, how he could ever know that he had been forgiven for his terrible sins. The *Baal Shem* told him that when someone came along and told this very story to him, it would be the sign from Heaven that he had finally found atonement, and his sincere *teshuva* had been accepted.

Now everything was clear to the storyteller. Why the *Baal Shem* had told him to go around telling stories about him in the first place, and why this man had been paying for stories about him.[ט]

❁ ❁ ❁ ❁ ❁ ❁ ❁ ❁ ❁ ❁ ❁ ❁

פרשת בהעלתך

Parshas Behaaloscha

ויעש כן אהרן
'And Aharon did so'
(Bamidbar 8:3)

Rashi *zt"l* quotes from *Sifri* that this is to tell the praise of Aharon, that he did not change -- meaning; from what Hashem had said to do.

But there is a very fundamental question that many ask on this: How is the *passuk* praising Aharon? Would he have deviated from Hashem's Command, *Chas v'Shalom*?!

The **Ramban** *zt"l* explains like this: Even though the service of the *Menorah* was allowed to be done by Aharon's sons, as the verse tells us, he himself did it all the days of his life.

The third *Gerrer* Rebbe -- the *Sfas Emes*, **HaRav Yehuda Aryeh Leib Alter** *zt"l* suggests another understanding: It is the way of people that at first, when we do a *Mitzvah*, we are inspired, but after some time, the inspiration fades. However, with Aharon HaKohen, he 'did not change' -- but always performed the Commandment of lighting the *Menorah* like he did the first time.[א]

And very similarly, **HaRav Avraham Schorr** *shlit"a* says that Aharon HaKohen never did the service of the *Menorah* out of habit or rote; he didn't change -- always doing it with passion and fire.[ב]

Another explanation is posed by **Rebbe Simcha Bunim of Peshischa** *zt"l*: Even though he merited this great thing, Aharon HaKohen 'didn't change' in <u>his own eyes</u>, in that he didn't look at himself as great and become haughty in any way, but rather remained the same humble person he was before.[1]

And finally, I would like to suggest, very simply, that the truth is that every time we do the right thing, and we don't deviate from what Hashem has told us, that is something very great. So indeed, the verse is certainly telling the praise of Aharon, for it is a <u>great</u> accolade to say that he *'did so'*, like Hashem had commanded.

ואתנה את הלוים נתנים לאהרן ולבניו מתוך בני ישראל לעבד את עבדת בני ישראל באהל מועד ולכפר על בני ישראל ולא יהיה בבני ישראל נגף בגשת בני ישראל אל הקדש

'And I have given the Leviim, given to Aharon and to his sons from the midst of the Children of Israel to perform (lit. serve) the service of the Children of Israel in the Tent of Meeting, and to atone upon the Children of Israel, and there will not be in the Children of Israel a plague when the Children of Israel approach to the Sanctuary.'
(Bamidbar 8:19)

R ashi *zt"l* quotes from *Midrash Bereishis Rabbah*: Five times it says *Bnei Yisroel* in this verse, to tell us their dearness to Hashem. For, mention of them is repeated in one verse like the number of the Five *Chumashim* of the Torah.

Says **HaRav Dov Weinberger** *zt"l*: Many ask; why specifically here are *Bnei Yisroel* compared to the Five *Chumashim* of the Torah? And also, we may wonder; why is the wording 'Five <u>Chumashim</u> of the Torah' used, instead of, let's say, portions, or orders, like the *Mishnah*?

It appears, says Rav Weinberger, that specifically this language of the 'Five *Chumashim* of the Torah' was chosen, because every *Chumash* stands by itself, but yet, they are all only one fifth of the Torah, and cannot possibly be separated from any of the other *Chumashim*. This is just like with the banners for the different Tribes, in that each and every Tribe stood on its own, but wasn't separated from the greater community.

It is the same thing here. Even though the *Leviim* were chosen to be, in a sense, elevated above the rest of the *Bnei Yisroel*, and to perform the special Service, and the *Bnei Yisroel* agreed to this, nevertheless, the elevation of the *Leviim* was *'from the midst of the Bnei Yisroel'*. Meaning that they all remained attached to one another. And now we see the beautiful comparison to the **חמשה חומשי תורה**.[ד]

ויאמרו האנשים ההמה אליו אנחנו טמאים לנפש אדם
למה נגרע לבלתי הקריב את קרבן השם במעדו בתוך בני
ישראל

*'Why should we be diminished to not bring the
offering of Hashem in its proper time, in the midst of
the Children of Israel?'*
(Bamidbar 9:7)

The Torah tells us that there were men who were ritually impure through contact with a human corpse at Pesach time, and therefore, they couldn't bring the *Pesach*-offering at its proper juncture. Moshe Rabbeinu came before Hashem, and He told him the law of *Pesach Sheini* -- that, if, for some very compelling reason, a person couldn't offer the *Pesach*-offering on the 14th of Nissan, then they would have a make-up day to offer it. One month later, on the 14th of Iyar.

We find something wondrous, says **HaRav Shimshon Dovid Pincus** *zt"l*, with the Pesach-offering; something that is not found with any other *Mitzvah* of the Torah, and it is *Pesach Sheini*.

It is known that with the *Mitzvos* that have a certain specific time for their performance, that if that time passes, and you didn't do the *Mitzvah*, then you lost that opportunity, and there isn't a makeup period.

Unique in this respect is the *Korban Pesach*,[16] which has a make-up period, and someone who was in a state of ritual impurity, for example, and therefore couldn't offer it in its proper time, is able to bring it in the coming month, on the 14th of Iyar, which is called *Pesach Sheini*.

We learn from this, expounds Rav Pincus, a great principle: It happens often that we miss an opportunity to grow in Torah and *Avodas Hashem*. But if we come with the argument of the people who weren't able to offer the *Korban Pesach* in its proper time, *'why should be diminished?'* -- why should I not merit this? -- and we try and toil to fill in what we are deficient in, then we can merit a *Pesach Sheini*, as it were. Even if we began late, or weren't educated in such in our youth.

It isn't for naught that **Chazal** emphasize that one of the greatest *Tannaim* to ever live was Rabbi Akiva, who, until the age of forty, was totally unlearned in Torah. But when he was awakened, and took it upon himself to be devoted to Torah, he wasn't content with just a little bit of it. He put all his strengths into it, until he became the great Rabbi Akiva! We learn from this that it is within our capabilities to fill in the deficiency of our younger days, even to a very high level![17]

---

[16] Although there are other things with "make-up" times, *Pesach Sheini* is unique, in a certain way.

[17] Of course, in no way does this mean that if we already know better, we have an excuse to act however we wish while we are young. It is speaking after-the-fact.

Sometimes, one who sees that they are lacking in levels, *middos*, etc. that they wish they would achieve, might think to themsleves, "If only I could be born anew, then I would be able to ascend in Torah." But the truth is that if we begin to learn in the proper way right now, and try to really understand the studies, and review them so that we remember them, certainly we will make progress in Torah. And the same goes in all other areas of *Avodah*. And even if we aren't young anymore, it isn't too late!

If we sincerely desire and try to reach higher, Hashem will give us that second chance and opportunity, and enable us to attain what we didn't, or couldn't, before.ⁿ

✽ ✽ ✽ ✽ ✽ ✽ ✽ ✽ ✽ ✽ ✽ ✽ ✽

והאיש אשר הוא טהור ובדרך לא היה

'And the man that will be pure, and was not on the road'
(Bamidbar 9:13)

One of the *Chassidishe Rebbes* interpreted an incredible lesson from these words: The person who is haughty, and thinks of themselves as pure -- that person is not on the right *derech*. . . ¹

✽ ✽ ✽ ✽ ✽ ✽ ✽ ✽ ✽ ✽ ✽ ✽ ✽

על פי השם יחנו ועל פי השם יסעו

'Upon the Word of Hashem, they encamped, and upon the Word of Hashem, they journeyed.'
(Bamidbar 9:20)

In these words, teaches **HaRav Yosef Chaim Chazani** *zt"l*, we see a hint to a great lesson: Regarding everything we plan to do, we should say about it *'im yirtzeh Hashem'* or something similar. And when we do achieve what we were hoping to, or come to a place we wanted, we should say a praise to Hashem, like *'Baruch Hashem'*. [1]

ויסעו מהר השם
'And they journeyed from the Mountain of Hashem'
(Bamidbar 10:33)

The Sages derive[18] that, unfortunately, this phrase implies that *Klal Yisroel* turned away from following Hashem. *Tosafos*[19] brings the words of the *Midrash*,[20] which says that we fled from *Har Sinai* like a child from school, because we had gotten a lot of *Mitzvos*, and we were afraid that Hashem would give us more.

Asks **HaRav Yerucham Levovitz** *zt"l*; how could *Klal Yisroel* have run away from *Har Sinai*? Don't we read explicitly that we only traveled by the Word of Hashem?

---

[18] *Shabbos* 116a

[19] *Ibid.*

[20] *Yilamdeinu*

And furthermore, how could this lofty generation, the *Dor Deiah*, have done such a thing?!

Explains Rav Levovitz; we must say that what **Chazal** mean to tell us is that when Hashem told us to travel from *Har Sinai*, we left too quickly. We had too much enthusiasm to leave. We should have, yes, felt excited to fulfill the command of Hashem to journey, but also felt like we wanted to stay so badly at this place where we received the holy Torah.

When you are finished a learning session, don't, figuratively, close your *sefer* so fast. Don't just leave behind what you learned when you are done. When it comes *bein hazmanim*, don't be so excited to leave *yeshiva*. Such things, as we see from **Chazal**, are, in a sense, turning away from Hashem. We must literally cling to the holy Torah, and never want to leave its embrace.ח

ויקרא את שם המקום ההוא קברות התאוה כי שם
קברו את העם המתאוים
'And he called the name of that place Kivros HaTaavah, for there they buried the people who were craving.'
(Bamidbar 11:34)

There is a very valuable lesson to be learned from the name '*Kivros HaTaavah*', which literally means 'Graves of the Desire':

The **Alter of Novhardok** *zt"l* compares the *yetzer hara* to a joker who tricked someone to put a handkerchief over his eyes and pretend to be blind so that he would be let enter a health institution and get a bed designated for patients, and good meals. The man did so and he loved it! After some time, the joker took the "blind" man to the middle of the marketplace, and told him to undress, because here was a lovely river, and he should go for a swim and enjoy himself! The man believed him, and, not being able to see where he really was because he was wearing the handkerchief over his eyes, quickly took off his clothes to jump into the water.

At that moment, the joker approached the man, pulled off his blindfold, grabbed his clothing, and fled. The "blind" man was left standing naked in the middle of the marketplace, mocked by all the townspeople.

So it is, says the *Alter*, with the *yetzer hara*, who blinds the innocent, and promises them many sweet and pleasant promises. But eventually, the person finds themselves naked. Naked of all the fantasies and promises of the *yetzer hara*, and naked of ethical and spiritual perfection -- and they recognize their shame.[20]

This is one of the things alluded to in the name '*Kivros HaTaavah*'. The Torah says in *Parshas Eikev*,[21] when speaking of conquering the nations residing in Israel: '*And you will consume all the peoples that Hashem your G-d gives to*

---

[21] Devarim 7:16

you. . . and you shall not serve their gods, for it is a snare for you.'

What is a snare? It is something that catches and traps things! The Torah is not only telling us what not to do when we came into *Eretz Yisroel*, but it is giving us advice for life: *Avodah zarah* -- and all evil things -- although they might at times seem pleasurable or good, do not help us nor make our lives better. On the contrary, they try to lure us in and catch us, and ruin both our lives in this world and the Next. Someone who, *Chas v'Shalom*, just runs after their desires will eventually be buried by them.

❀ ❀ ❀ ❀ ❀ ❀ ❀ ❀ ❀ ❀ ❀ ❀ ❀ ❀

ותדבר מרים ואהרן במשה . . . וישמע השם
**'And Miriam and Aharon spoke against Moshe. . .
and Hashem heard.'**
(Bamidbar 12:1-2)

The emphasis of the phrase *'and Hashem heard'*, said my dear brother, **Reb Eliezer Yosef**, may he live and be well, is a reminder to us that Hashem <u>always</u> hears when we are talking. So we have to be very careful to guard our tongues, as Hashem hears everything we say.

❀ ❀ ❀ ❀ ❀ ❀ ❀ ❀ ❀ ❀ ❀ ❀ ❀ ❀

ותדבר מרים ואהרן במשה . . . וישמע השם . . . ויחר אף השם בם . . . והנה מרים מצרעת

***'And Miriam and Aharon spoke against Moshe. . .
And the anger of Hashem burned against them. . .
And behold! Miriam was stricken with Tzaraas'***
(Bamidbar 12:1, 9-10)

Why, the question is asked, was Miriam punished more than Aharon was, when they both spoke against Moshe Rabbeinu?

Answers **Rabbeinu Bachya** *zt"l*; Miriam spoke the criticism, but Aharon acknowledged it, or was just silent [instead of protesting]. Therefore, although Aharon was also punished, as we see that *'Hashem became very angry against <u>them</u>'*, Miriam, who initiated the *lashon hara*, her punishment was publicized, but Aharon's wasn't.[22]

⇜⇛

I felt the need to bring here the beautiful words that **Rashi** *zt"l* quotes from *Midrash Tanchuma* and *Sifri*: If Miriam, who did not intend to denigrate Moshe, was punished such, then all the more so one who relates something with the intention of denigrating their fellow [would be punished harshly].

* * * * * * * * * * * *

והאיש משה עניו מאד מכל האדם אשר על פני האדמה

---

[22] See similarly **Ibn Ezra**, and also **Daas Zikeinim MiBaalei Tosafos.**

> *'And the man Moshe was very humble, more than every person that is on the face of the earth.'*
> **(Bamidbar 12:3)**

Says the *Ksav Sofer*, HaRav Avraham Shmuel Binyamin Sofer *zt"l*: Some people act like they are humble and tolerating of everything, in order that others will praise them that they are humble and such. But the true humble person is actually humble; without any strategies, etc. behind their humility.

How can we recognize, though, which category of the above two someone falls into? Whether they are actually humble, or just putting on an act so that people will praise them for being humble? The answer is, if someone behaves in a humble manner, and even when they hear others saying that they are a *baal gaavah*, they still remain silent and tolerate it, then we see that they are truly humble.

Based on this, says the *Ksav Sofer*, we can explain the situation with Moshe Rabbeinu: Moshe Rabbeinu always displayed signs of humility, and he accepted and endured hard things many times, but still one might have suspected him of, *Chas v'Shalom*, acting like that so people would praise him that he is so humble, and everything like that. But since he was spoken against, and accused, in a way, of being haughty and taking grandeur for himself, and still he endured this and was silent, not responding to the insult, it proved that he was truly humble. And regarding this, the *passuk* praises him, as now it was clear that his humility was true.'

והאיש משה עניו מאד מכל האדם אשר על פני האדמה

'And the man Moshe was very humble, more than every person that is on the face of the earth.'
(Bamidbar 12:3)

Tells us **Reb Meshulam Gross** *zt"l*: There are different types of humble people. One kind is someone who is humble when they are sitting in their house, and take a spiritual accounting of themselves, and see how "small" they are compared to HaKadosh Baruch Hu. However, when they go out among others, and they see the learning, *Davening*, and *Avodah* in general, of those people, then they feel elevated above them, because they are on a higher level than them.

But there is another kind of person, who is far humbler than the first we mentioned, who, even though they are a great *Talmid Chacham*, and very pious, etc. still has self-effacement before all people, even if those people "aren't as good as them."

This was the quality of Moshe Rabbeinu, says Reb Gross, and this is what the *passuk* means when it says that he was humble, literally *'from every person'* -- for, not only when he was by himself was he humble, but even when he went outside, he was humble before all people.[א]

Similarly, **HaRav Moshe Shternbuch** *shlit"a* quotes that he saw in a *sefer* a story related in the name of **HaRav Meir Shapiro** *zt"l*:

One time, **HaRav Yonasan Eibeshutz** *zt"l* was visiting a certain town on *Erev* Yom Kippur, and he overheard a Jew reciting supplications before Hashem from the depths of his heart. "Hashem, before I was formed, I was not worthy, and now that I have been formed, it is as if I was not formed. I am dirt in my life, all the more so in my death." **השם עד שלא נוצרתי איני כדאי ועכשיו שנוצרתי כאילו לא נוצרתי. עפר אני בחיי קל וחומר במיתתי**

Rav Yonasan was very moved and inspired by this man's sincere prayers, and was very happy that he would get to *daven* together with him on Yom Kippur.

The next day, this man was honored with the fourth *Aliyah – Revi'i*. But he complained very much about it, until he raised his voice and said, "Why did So-and-so get *Shlishi*, and I only read at *Revi'i*?!"

Rav Yonasan wondered about this man's behavior, and he asked him, "Yesterday, did you not say before HaKadosh Baruch Hu ''*I am dirt in my life*', and how can you seek honor for yourself?" The man replied, "Yesterday, when I was standing before HaKadosh Baruch Hu I said '*I am dirt in my life*', for what am I before HaKadosh Baruch Hu? But my importance rises much higher than the Jew who got *Shlishi*!"

The greatness of Moshe Rabbeinu's humility was its authenticity and completeness. Even, for example, when he was speaking to those amongst *Klal Yisroel* who were complaining, he said (Shemos 16:7) *"What are we?"* Even compared to them, Moshe Rabbeinu didn't think of himself as important or better.יג

Another wonderful explanation I heard on this verse comes from **Rebbe Shalom Dov Ber of Lubavitch** *zt"l*: Moshe Rabbeinu, he says, looked forward to the future generations, and saw our times. And he saw what incredible new *nisyonos* (trials) we would face, and that still, at least some of the Jewish People are holding on and remaining steadfast to Hashem and His Torah! And Moshe thought to himself that he couldn't even compare to such amazing people. He was humble literally **מכל האדם** *'from all people'*!יד

❧Maasim Tovim❧

על פי השם יחנו ועל פי השם יסעו
'*Upon the Word of Hashem, they encamped, and upon the Word of Hashem, they journeyed.*'
(Bamidbar 9:20)

One day, when **HaRav Chaim Kanievsky** *shlit"a* was young, the Kanievsky's washing machine stopped working. The technician said that one of the machine's parts had broken, and they needed to buy a new spare part from a store in Tel Aviv.

Rav Chaim's sister was sent to Tel Aviv to buy the part. She decided that while in the city, she would take care of another matter as well.

"I'm going to Tel Aviv to buy a part for the washing machine." She told their father, the **Steipler Gaon, HaRav Yaakov Yisroel Kanievsky** *zt"l*. The *Steipler* added, "You should say, '*im yirtzeh Hashem*'!"

After an exhausting trip, Rav Chaim's sister returned home. While she had, *Baruch Hashem*, managed to complete her other errand, she had not managed to buy the spare part for the washing machine.

From that day on, Rav Chaim and his sister paid attention to a "small", but very significant "spare part", that directly affects one's success, and, if absent, *Chas v'Shalom*, seems to remove success. From that day on, they understood to say '*im yirtzeh Hashem*' to every future action, as their father did.ᵈⁱ

והאיש משה עניו מאד מכל האדם אשר על פני האדמה

> **'And the man Moshe was very humble, more than
> every person that is on the face of the earth.'**
> **(Bamidbar 12:3)**

Once, **HaRav Yitzchok Blazer** *zt"l*, fondly known as **Reb Itzele Peterburger**, went to a meeting together with many other *Gedolim* and *Rabbonim* in St. Petersburg, Russia. Among the *Gedolim* present at this gathering was **HaRav Yosef Dov Soloveitchik** *zt"l*, *Rav* of Brisk, and he posed a very sharp and difficult question in the name of his son, **HaRav Chaim** *zt"l*. The *Rabbonim* debated back and forth, each one giving beautiful explanations, which were then challenged, among much wonderful Torah give-and-take -- all of them displaying incredible depth and breadth of knowledge in the holy Torah.

In the end, Rav Yosef Dov answered the question with two explanations; one of his own, and one said by his son, Rav Chaim, which amazed everyone present.

All throughout this, though, one of the *Rabbonim* at the meeting had not so much as opened his mouth to speak, as if he did not even understand the discussions. That *Rav* was Reb Itzele. And Rav Yosef Dov wondered about this -- "Is this the man they say is a great, scholarly person?" he thought.

When Rav Yosef Dov returned to his home, he asked for Reb Itzele's *sefer*, **Pri Yitzchok**, to be brought to him, so that he could see for himself what level Reb Itzele was holding on. Upon looking into the *sefer*, Rav Yosef Dov found, to his wonderment, the question of his son, Rav Chaim, and also both his answer, and that of his son! Rav Yosef Dov was so impressed by Reb Itzele, and he called out, "How great is the humility of Rav Yitzchok!"טז

✺ ✺ ✺ ✺ ✺ ✺ ✺ ✺ ✺ ✺ ✺ ✺ ✺

פרשת שלח

Parshas Shelach

שלח לך אנשים
'Send for yourself men'
(Bamidbar 13:2)

Rashi *zt"l* brings the question from *Midrash Tanchuma*; why is the section about the *Meraglim* (spies) put in close proximity to the section dealing with when Miriam spoke *lashon hara* against Moshe, which was at the very end of last *Parsha*? Because she was punished for speaking badly about her brother, and these *Meraglim* saw this, but yet, they didn't learn the lesson [and slandered *Eretz Yisroel*].

HaRav Chaim Shmuelevitz *zt"l* expands beautifully on this: What we see and what happens to us in our life is a direct message to us. It is not just a coincidence. And we must apply the lesson to ourselves personally, because it is intended directly to us! This was one of the mistakes of *Meraglim*; they didn't apply the *mussar* they saw to themselves, and therefore, they came to fail in that very area.ℵ

שלח לך אנשים
'Send for yourself men'
(Bamidbar 13:2)

Says *Mori v'Rebbe*, **HaRav Elyakim Rosenblatt** *zt"l*, (adapted from a *shmuess* of **HaRav Leib Chasman** *zt"l* and **HaRav Chaim Shmuelevitz** *zt"l*): In this *Parsha* the Torah speaks of the spies who were sent to explore *Eretz Yisroel*, to see if it can be conquered. The Torah describes how very extraordinary these spies were. They were all "*Anashim*", which **Rashi** *zt"l* explains to mean "distinguished" people. Among them were people even greater than Kalev and Yehoshua. Such were the great people who were chosen to explore *Eretz Yisroel*.

They returned from exploring the land at the end of forty days and delivered an evil report about the Holy Land. "We will never be able to conquer it because the people in *Eretz Yisroel* are stronger "ממנו" than us. **Chazal** interpret the word "ממנו" to mean stronger than Him, meaning Hashem. The Spies were saying that the inhabitants of *Eretz Yisroel* were even stronger than Hashem, *Chas v'Shalom*! To make such a statement, claiming that Hashem was incapable of helping them, means that they were "כופרים בעיקר", they failed to believe in Hashem's Omnipotence.

But how was it possible that such great and holy people could sink to such a low level, not even believing in Hashem properly -- and further, in a mere forty days?

The **Mesilas Yesharim** brings from the **Zohar HaKadosh** that the spies had a tremendous temptation for honor. They were afraid that the high positions they had attained, being princes of Israel, were only temporary, enduring only while they were in the Wilderness. At the time they would enter *Eretz Yisroel* -- fully comprehending its holiness -- they were afraid that they would be unable to retain their high positions anymore and they would be replaced by others. This pursuit of honor was so much a focus of their lives that anything jeopardizing this end, namely their entering *Eretz Yisroel*, had to be prevented from becoming a reality. This desire for honor distorted their vision. They did not want to enter *Eretz Yisroel*, nor

67

did they even want to believe that Hashem had the ability to help them enter into the Holy Land.

Furthermore, this position that they had, according to the **Baal HaTurim**, was not even so grandiose, as they were only leaders of fifty people. Even that small honor which they had garnered, and wanted so much to retain, distorted their vision.

We see here the devastation caused by people motivated by the desire for honor. Uppermost in their minds was the thought -- "we must retain our positions of leadership." All other thoughts, such as that *Eretz Yisroel* could be conquered and that Hashem could bring them into the Holy Land, fell by the wayside. This desire for honor totally clouded their ability to see the truth.

We see from here that even such great and holy people are not immune from serious character flaws. They can have faults -- being guilty of coveting honor -- which can bring about much destruction. Even the greatest people have to guard themselves, because they can fall into such a trap. And, of course, all the more so we must be on guard…

❋ ❋ ❋ ❋ ❋ ❋ ❋ ❋ ❋ ❋ ❋ ❋ ❋

ויקרא משה להושע בן נון יהושע
'And Moshe called Hoshea bin Nun, Yehoshua.'
(Bamidbar 13:16)

Rashi *zt"l* tells us (from *Gemara Sotah*) the significance of adding the letter *yud* to the beginning of Yehoshua's name: Moshe Rabbeinu prayed for him that Hashem (י‑ה) should save him from the counsel of the bad spies.

The question is asked; why did Moshe Rabbeinu pray only on behalf of Yehoshua, and not for Calev, nor any of the other *Meraglim*?

HaRav Meir Simcha HaKohen of Dvinsk *zt"l* explains that the *Bnei Yisroel* were afraid of Amalek *ym"s* after the war with them. Regarding this, the *Meraglim* said, '*Amalek dwells in the land of the south.*' And Moshe Rabbeinu was afraid that if the people were to hear also from Yehoshua -- the person who waged the war against Amalek -- some expression of fear of them, then all hope would be lost. . . Therefore, he specifically prayed for Yehoshua.[א]

※

In a different take, the **Kehillas Yitzchok** elucidates that there are two different types of sins: The first are those transgressions that the person who does them knows that this thing isn't good, but it is just hard to not do it. The second type are sins which the *yetzer hara* dresses up in the "clothing" of a *Mitzvah*, trying to trick us into doing them, and making us think we are doing something good all the while! This second type can be harder to refrain from doing than the first.

Now, the *Zohar* tells us that the *Meraglim* were worried that Moshe Rabbeinu was going to appoint new leaders in their stead when they entered *Eretz Yisroel*. But even so -- that they had some interests in the matter -- since, as we see in the *Midrash*, these men were great and righteous people, Moshe Rabbeinu thought that they would overcome the temptation to such a plain sin, as they obviously knew what intentions would be behind their slander of the Land.

But as for Yehoshua, when Eldad and Meidad were prophesying, according to one opinion in the *Gemara*, they foretold that Moshe would die, and Yehoshua would enter into *Eretz Yisroel*, and, as we know, Yehoshua got zealously upset at them. Therefore, Moshe Rabbeinu was worried that Yehoshua -- yes, Yehoshua -- thinking that it was a *Mitzvah* in this case, would on purpose mess up the spying mission, and bring a bad report about the Land, so that the *Bnei Yisroel* wouldn't wish to ascend there, and thus, Moshe would remain alive. Therefore, he prayed for Yehoshua that he not fall into this *yetzer-hara*-trap of a fake *Mitzvah*. [23]

✻ ✻ ✻ ✻ ✻ ✻ ✻ ✻ ✻ ✻ ✻ ✻ ✻ ✻

ויאמר עלה נעלה וירשנו אתה כי יכול נוכל לה

'And he [Calev] said: "We shall surely ascend and take possession of it [Eretz Yisroel], for we are surely able to do it!"'

(Bamidbar 13:30)

---

[23] See also in *Chofetz Chaim al HaTorah* on this matter.

Says the *Piaseczna Rebbe, HaRav Kalonymous Kalman Shapira zt"l*: The *Meraglim* presented their arguments in a very logical fashion. The people inhabiting the land are very strong; the cities are fortified; etc. Logically we wouldn't be able to beat them! So then why did Calev not answer them accordingly -- contradicting their words with logical arguments? Why did he just say *'we shall surely ascend, etc.'*?

Answers the *Piaseczna Rebbe* beautifully, this is how our *Emunah* in Hashem needs to be: Not just when, logically and by the "natural order" of things we can see a way that our salvation will come must we believe in Hashem that He will save us. But also, at a time that we <u>don't</u> see any logical and natural path to our being saved, we still must have faith that Hashem will save us.

Various descriptions which the *Meraglim* gave were factual; yes, the people who were dwelling in *Eretz Yisroel* were strong; it's true, the cities were fortified. But in a scary and bleak-looking situation like that, the *Bnei Yisroel* -- and we – had, and have, to understand that although this might be a reality, nevertheless, HaKadosh Baruch Hu is above the boundaries of "nature", and He can save us no matter what, and we must believe such. *'We shall surely ascend,'* said Calev. Such faith can actually bring our salvation.[7]

ויאמר עלה נעלה וירשנו אתה כי יכול נוכל לה

'And he [Calev] said: "We shall surely ascend and take possession of it [Eretz Yisroel], for we are surely able to do it!"'
(Bamidbar 13:30)

In this *Parsha*, we read the famous account of the dispatchment of leaders to "spy" out *Eretz Yisroel*. And as we know, they did not bring back a very favorable report for the Land, and the *Bnei Yisroel* became discouraged.

One of the big things that the *Meraglim* spoke of was how much larger and stronger the nations residing in the Land at that time were than them. There were giants! But yet we see an amazing thing; Calev said that, *'we can surely go up and take possession of it'*! And indeed, had the Jews had faith in the Ribbono Shel Olam, and listened to Him to go up and take possession of *Eretz Yisroel*, they <u>would</u> have been victorious.

This teaches us an incredible thing: No challenge is insurmountable. Every trial that we run up against in our lives, no matter how big, we <u>can</u> overcome, with the Help of Hashem. We must put in our efforts and place our faith and trust in Him, and He will graciously help us do things that we might have doubted we could accomplish.

מראשית ערסתיכם תתנו להשם תרומה
'From the first of your dough you shall give to Hashem a contribution'

(Bamidbar 15:21)

Based somewhat on a teaching from the **Rebbe Reb Zusha** *zt"l*, the **Maggid of Kozhnitz**, (**Rebbe Yisroel Haupstein** *zt"l*), explains this verse in a beautiful, homiletical way:

It is very easy to think "I'm still young; there's still time to do whatever I want. When I get old, I'll return to serve Hashem. But for now, I'll 'rejoice in my youth.'"[24]

But this *passuk* precludes this notion, and tells us that it is extremely important and fundamental that we serve Hashem when we are young as well, sanctifying *'from the "first"'* of our strength, which we have to a fuller extent at that juncture in life.ח

והיה לכם לציצית וראיתם אותו וזכרתם את כל מצות השם

'And it shall be for you as Tzitzis; and you shall see it, and you will remember all the Commandments of Hashem. . .'
(Bamidbar 15:39)

The truth is that many contingencies of true joy, and many things overall, are in large part dependent upon 'slowing things down.' Not running through life.[25]

---

[24] See *Koheles* 11:9.

[25] See **Positive Pointers**, p. 3.

For example, if we learn Torah and *Daven* robotically and just rush through them, will we really feel the beauty, *Simcha* and amazing privilege of them? And how can we possibly see the tremendous kindnesses of HaKadosh Baruch Hu everywhere if we are merely going quickly through everything? And what about contemplating our actions, etc.?

This concept is taught in the above *passuk*: We are told that we are supposed to see the *Tzitzis*, and they will remind us of all the *Mitzvos* of Hashem. Perhaps the only way to do this is if we would but slow down a little. If we do not slow ourselves down to a certain extent, then we could see our *Tzitzis* many, many times, but not think of anything from them!

But *oy va voy*, many have such a tough and busy schedule, that, how can we not rush? We have to be at some place by 11:00 AM, and the drive takes such-and-such amount of minutes. Yanke'le is running late for school. The possibilities are nearly endless. So how can we "slow down"? How can we not rush through life?

The answer to this important question really is left to all of us to contemplate for our own personal lives and situations. But I would like to propose one answer, and that is that the tool for this is our mind. Hashem has granted us the incredible capability that even if we are on a very tight schedule or truthfully in a rush; within our <u>minds</u> we can still be moving at a regular pace. We can still be thinking clearly and not rushing. Of course, this is not a simple thing to do. But, as other things, we must learn *Mussar*, etc. and work on ourselves, trying to improve until we reach such a point.

והיה לכם לציצית וראיתם אותו וזכרתם את כל מצות השם

'And it shall be for you as Tzitzis; and you shall see it, and you will remember all the Commandments of Hashem. . .'
(Bamidbar 15:39)

Notes the **Baal HaTurim** *zt"l* that the *Gematria* (numerical value) of the word **ציצית** is 600. Add the eight strings and five sets of knots of each tassel, and we come out to a total of 613, like the total of the *Mitzvos* of the Torah!

∾Maasim Tovim∾

ועשו להם ציצת
'And they shall make for themselves Tzitzis'
(Bamidbar 15:38)

One time -- often told to be right before he passed away -- the **Vilna Gaon** *zt"l* said to his *talmidim* "How good it is for a person to be in this world!" And he explained as follows: "If, when a person comes to the World to Come, he would ask to be let do just one more

Mitzvah in order to attain a big and nice portion there, he wouldn't be able to. Yet, here, when he is in this world, he is able to rise up to a high level -- to the point of being able to greet the *Shechinah*! An example of this is the *Mitzvah* of *Tzitzis*, about which **Chazal** tell us that one who is careful in this *Mitzvah* will merit to see the *Shechinah*! And down here in this World, one can attain this exaltedness with just a tiny amount of money!"[1]

⋙⋘

ועשו להם ציצת
'And they shall make for themselves Tzitzis'
(Bamidbar 15:38)

There was a regular *yeshiva bochur* in *Eretz Yisroel* -- let's call him Levi -- who one day fell ill. After visiting the doctor and having checkups for some time, there was no improvement in his health. Eventually he was diagnosed with a certain malady which all dread from just hearing the mention of it, may Hashem have mercy! He was to begin at once a series of treatments.

After checking in to the hospital, he was given a set of sterile clothing. As he was about to start treatment the nurse noticed that he was wearing his *Tzitzis* over his hospital clothing. She told him that this was against hospital rules to wear anything else other than what the hospital specifically cleans and sterilizes. But Levi was adamant to wear his *Tzitzis*. The nurse refused to let him into the ward and told him to wait outside until he agreed to remove his personal clothes.

Levi was undeterred and refused to bend. He would not give up this beautiful *Mitzvah* so quickly. He felt that the *Tzitzis* were his 'life jacket' and during such trying times he would hold onto them with his dear life. So he sat outside the ward waiting patiently until the nurse would bend. He certainly was not going to give in.

After waiting for three whole hours the professor of the ward walked past and noticed Levi sitting outside in his hospital gown. He asked him what he was doing there and for whom he was waiting. Levi explained his problem and that he was patiently waiting for the nurse to allow him in while wearing his *Tzitzis*. The professor left and entered the ward. After some time he emerged totally enthusiastic and called Levi over to him. Levi wondered as to what he was so excited about. Before he had a chance to ask, the professor was first to speak. He told Levi that to begin with, he should enter and receive the necessary treatment. He was permitted to keep his *Tzitzis*, as he had sorted it out with the head nurse. Only after he was comfortably settled and treated, would the professor agree to reveal what had happened that got him so excited.

After Levi had been treated, the professor came to visit and check on him. With tears in his eyes, he told Levi that although he was not an observant Jew, nevertheless he had met Hashem, as it were, today with his very own eyes. After having met Levi outside the ward, he had entered and checked out what was going on and to hear first-hand from the nurse her side of the story. He checked his medical records and noticed that the nurse had made a grave error and had planned to give Levi the wrong treatment. If he would not have been stubborn about keeping the *Mitzvah* of *Tzitzis*, he most probably would not be around anymore by the time the professor would have entered the ward three hours later. "Your stubbornness has saved your life!" he remarked emotionally.

The happy ending of this story is, that when it was eventually printed a couple of years later in the *sefer* of **HaRav Yitzchok Zilberstein** *shlit"a* and made famous, the publishers received a phone call from Levi himself. Firstly, he testified to the authenticity of the story. Secondly, he added that he was completely cured and, in the meantime was happily married, against all the doctors' expectations.[1]

פרשת קרח

Parshas Korach

ויקח קרח בן יצהר בן קהת בן לוי. . .
*'And Korach, son of Yitzhar, son of Kehas, son of
Levi, took. . .'*
(Bamidbar 16:1)

We know from **Chazal**, as brought by **Rashi** *zt"l*, that Korach was upset that he was not appointed as Kohen Gadol, and furthermore, not even appointed as head of the Leviim, and he thus stirred up a rebellion against the authority of Moshe Rabbeinu, and in essence, against the authority of Hashem Himself.

If we see somebody getting something in life that we wanted; for example, a promotion or a certain position, we must realize that to complain would be to complain against Hashem, because He runs His world, and if we didn't get something, it is because He knew it wasn't best for us!

And to take this one step further, why should we complain, if we understood that everything that Hashem makes happen is truly for our benefit and for the best overall? Not getting whatever it is we wanted to get was good for us in this scenario, apparently. As **Rabbi Akiva** said,[26] *"Everything the Merciful One does, He does for the good."*

ויקח קרח בן יצהר בן קהת בן לוי. . .
'And Korach, son of Yitzhar, son of Kehas, son of Levi, took. . .'
(Bamidbar 16:1)

The *Mishnah* in *Pirkei Avos*[27] tells us: Every dispute that is *l'Sheim Shmayaim*, for the sake of Heaven, will endure. And one that is not for the sake of Heaven, will not endure. What is an example of a dispute that is for the sake of Heaven? The disputes of Hillel and Shammai. And what is an example of a dispute that was

---

[26] *Berachos* 60a.
[27] Ch. 5.

not for the sake of Heaven? The dispute of Korach and his entire assembly.

In what way does a dispute for the sake of Heaven endure, and in what way does one not for the sake of Heaven not endure?

Truthfully, it is quite clear: When people debate *l'Sheim Shamayim*, it means that they are not just arguing to prove their point. They are debating for a higher purpose, in order to bring out the truth of a matter, and each voicing Torah opinions. These words will endure forever; they are words of Torah! Furthermore, since they are debating *l'Sheim Shamayim*, there is a very good chance that in most cases, they will treat each other with respect, and not come to, *Chas v'Shalom*, try to insult one another.[28]

But people who argue merely from their own opinions, for some selfish reason, whether it be to show that they are correct, and the other person is wrong, or whatever it may be, those words are not going to last. Where is the specialness in them? And will this argument even shed light on the truth, or will it just cause unnecessary strife and feelings of enmity between people?

Asks **HaRav Yehuda Lirma** *zt"l*, why does the *Mishnah* not say 'the dispute of Korach and his entire assembly *with*

---

[28] See *Ye'aros D'vash vol. 2, Drush 1* and **Anaf Eitz Avos** to this *Mishnah*.

Moshe and Aharon'? Afterall, Moshe and Aharon also disagreed with him, and it's not like Moshe didn't dispute him!

However, he explains beautifully that the *Mishnah* could not have said thus, as it is giving an example of an argument which was not for the sake of Heaven, and the arguing which Moshe and Aharon did with Korach and his assembly surely <u>was</u> *l'Shem Shamayim*! The only people, therefore, whom it could mention, were Korach and his assembly, who weren't arguing *l'Shem Shamayim*.א

…

A similar, but different, question is asked by the **Noam Elimelech (Rebbe Elimelech of Lizhensk *zt"l*)**: Why does the *Mishnah* word it 'the dispute of Korach and his assembly'?

And he elucidates the matter as follows: As we find in **Rashi *zt"l***, all the 250 men of Korach's assembly also desired the position of Kohen Gadol, just like he did. Thus, we see that their hearts were also separated, and in disagreement. And this is what the wording of the *Mishnah* hints to us: The hearts of Korach and his assembly were all truthfully disjointed with one another. It was literally the dispute of Korach and his entire assembly!ב

רב לכם בני לוי
'It is much for you, sons of Levi!'
(Bamidbar 16:7)

Rashi *zt"l* brings from *Midrash Tanchuma*; why did Korach do the foolish thing that he did? The answer is that his eye, עינו, caused him to err, as he saw a chain of great people who would be descended from him, so therefore, he strove for an extremely exalted position for himself.

One of the sons of the *Ruzhiner Rebbe zt"l*, **HaRav Avraham Yaakov of Sadigur** *zt"l* noted the interesting singular language employed in the above **Chazal** that עינו, 'his <u>eye</u>' caused him to err, and not the plural עיניו, 'his eyes.'

And he explains beautifully: A person was given two eyes to see with. With one eye, they are supposed to (figuratively) see and recognize the greatness of Hashem, and with the other, they are supposed to perceive their own lowliness.

Korach was indeed a very good person at first; and, while the eye that was supposed to see the magnificence of HaKadosh Baruch Hu did so, and he definitely perceived that Hashem is very great, his other eye, the one with which a person should see their own smallness, he didn't employ properly, and he thought of himself as very high up. Now we understand the singular expression עינו: It was this <u>eye</u> which caused him to err in the way that he did.ᵃ

In the same vein, the *Orchos Tzaddikim*[29] tells us that *gaavah* (haughtiness) brings one to the pursuit of honor to lord it over people. And that, in fact, this was the source of the revolt of Korach and his assembly -- because of his *gaavah* -- for he sought to place himself high up, and to take a position of greatness that had not been given to him from Heaven. And because of this, he entered into strife, and from the strife emerged jealousy and hatred. And all of these are very lowly traits.

ויחר למשה מאד ויאמר אל השם. . . ולא הרעתי את אחד מהם

'And Moshe was very distressed,[30] *and he said to Hashem. . . "And I have not done bad to one of them."'*
(Bamidbar 16:15)

There are those, says **HaRav Meir Simcha HaKohen of Dvinsk** *zt"l*, who are praised as being humble, but really aren't very much so. To someone who is much lower than them in eminence, these people behave very, very nicely, and humble themselves before them. But when it comes to someone who is just as eminent as them, or perhaps more so -- where, if they were to humble themselves before them, people could legitimately think that it is not humility, but how they should be treating that

---

29 *Shaar HaGaavah.*

30 Translation follows **Rashi** *zt"l.*

person, because so-and-so is really higher than them in stature -- they push them away, degrade them, and glorify in their disgrace.

But Moshe Rabbeinu was not like this. He was actually, truly, humble! And therefore, he was never jealous of, or towards, people who were high up, or doing something that could have appeared like "competition", like Eldad and Meidad, for example, when they were prophesying in the camp. This is what the words *'I have not done bad to <u>one of them</u>'* mean: As we find in **Rashi** *zt"l*,[31] when the term 'one of them' is used in conjunction with a lot of people, it can denote the greatest individual among them. Even to such people, who were great in stature, Moshe Rabbeinu did not try to lessen their status -- on the contrary, he attempted to add to it and their honor.ᵀ

ותפתח הארץ את פיה ותבלע אתם
'And the earth opened its mouth, and swallowed them'
(Bamidbar 16:32)

HaRav Avigdor Miller *zt"l* brought out a nice, practical message from this episode: Why did the earth open its big mouth to swallow Korach? Because Korach opened his big mouth to speak against Moshe! So don't open your mouth if you shouldn't! Because even today the earth opens its mouth to bury people. Many are

---

[31] To Bereishis 26:10.

swallowed in an early grave because they opened their mouths to say the wrong things, or to get involved in things they shouldn't have. And what's even worse is that many are swallowed into *Gehenom*, just like Korach was.ה

❋ ❋ ❋ ❋ ❋ ❋ ❋ ❋ ❋ ❋ ❋ ❋ ❋ ❋

ולא יהיה כקרח וכעדתו
'And he should not be like Korach and like his assembly'
(Bamidbar 17:5)

Please, let us not be like Korach and his assembly. We mustn't cause unnecessary arguments and strife! Sometimes there will be differences of opinion, yes, but it doesn't have to become an argument, or much worse, lead to anger and frustration! And if we must dispute something, or debate, it must be *l'Shem Shamayim*, as we saw above. It is imperative to try to maintain peace.

In *Parshas Bechukosai*,[32] **Rashi** *zt"l* brings from **Chazal** that peace is equivalent to everything. And the last *Mishnah* in all of *Shas*, **Uktzin** 3:12 -- the last *Mishnah* in all of *Shas*, *Rabbosai!* -- tells us: *'Rabbi Shimon ben Chalafta said: HaKadosh Baruch Hu did not find a vessel to hold blessing for Yisroel, except for <u>peace</u>, like it says, 'Hashem will give strength to His People, Hashem will bless His People with peace.'*

---

[32] *Vayikra 26:6*

We find back in *Parshas Vayeira* the famous story of when the Angels in the guise of wayfarers came to Avraham Avinu and Sara Imeinu, and told them that they would bear a son. Sara laughed, commenting about her physical state, and saying that her husband was old. But when HaKadosh Baruch Hu asked Avraham Avinu about it, He left out the second part, and only mentioned that she had said that she was old. From here the Academy of Rabbi Yishmael (**Bava Metzia** 87a) says how great peace is, as even HaKadosh Baruch Hu changed the truth, to a certain extent,[33] for it! It is incumbent upon us to learn from Hashem's perfect ways, and go to great lengths to preserve peace!

The *Midrash*[34] stresses the importance of peace further: Great is peace, says the *Midrash*, for the entire world is only conducted with peace, and the Torah is entirely peace, as it says[35] '*Its ways are ways of pleasantness, and all its paths are peace*'.

The **Chofetz Chaim** *zt"l* writes[36] that if we could build the *Beis HaMikdash* right now, and we just needed lots of money for it, surely we would all give generously and happily whatever we could, in order that we, too, would have a share in the *Beis HaMikdash*. However, says the

---

[33] Actually, if we look closely, Hashem merely refrained from telling the second thing Sara Imeinu said, but did not alter the truth, *Chas v'Shalom*, as her comments about herself essentially stated that she was old. See **Ramban** *zt"l* there.

[34] *Bamidbar Rabbah* ch. 21.

[35] *Mishlei* 3:17.

[36] *Shemiras HaLashon, vol. 2,* end of ch. 7.

Chofetz Chaim, to rebuild the *Beis HaMikdash*, we don't need to give any money. We only need to distance ourselves from the terrible sin of *lashon hara* and baseless hatred, and to take hold of the *middah* of peace, which will bring Mashiach and the rebuilding of the *Beis HaMikdash*! Speedily and in our days!

והנה פרח מטה אהרן לבית לוי ויצא פרח ויצץ ציץ ויגמל שקדים

'And behold! The staff of Aharon, of the House of Levi, blossomed; and it brought forth a blossom, and it sprouted a bud, and it grew almonds.'
(Bamidbar 17:23)

We can infer from this *passuk*, says **HaRav Moshe Feinstein** *zt"l*, that on Aharon's staff, the blossoms were left, as well as the almonds. In fact, the *Gemara* itself[37] implies this, as it says that the staff of Aharon was hidden away with its almonds <u>and</u> blossoms. And the **Tosafos Yeshanim** notes the difficulty, that once it had almonds, then, by definition, the blossoms would have fallen off already. But he brings that a miracle was performed, and the blossoms remained. Why, though, wonders Rav Moshe, did Hashem perform this miracle?

And he explains beautifully: Blossoms represent the things which bring us to the performance of a *Mitzvah*,

---

[37] *Yoma* 52b.

while the fruit -- the almonds, in this case, is like the actual act of the *Mitzvah* itself.

The remaining of the blossoms on the staff as well shows us that the "blossoms of holiness," meaning all the toil, and all the pain we might go through to perform a *Mitzvah* or learn Torah, never fades away or is lost. Unlike in mundane matters where we only get paid for the result of what we do, and not the effort we put into it, in spiritual matters, our efforts last forever, just like the *Mitzvah* itself, and Hashem rewards us for them as well!'

☞Maasim Tovim☜

ולא הרעתי את אחד מהם
'And I have not done bad to one of them.'
(Bamidbar 16:15)

*See our comment above from the **Meshech Chochmah** on this verse.*

HaRav Isser Zalman Meltzer *zt"l* used to give a weekly Talmudic lecture in his *yeshiva*. One of the students who usually remained silent during the lecture once spoke up and said, "The **Sfas Emes** explains this section differently than what was just said." Rav Meltzer, the *Rosh Yeshiva*, replied, "If the *Sfas Emes* explains the *Gemara* differently, I should really stop my lecture right away. But I ask of you a favor. I worked hard to prepare this lecture. Do me a *chesed* and give me permission to continue the lecture which I prepared with so much effort." This statement of the *Rosh Yeshiva* seemed a bit strange. Even if another scholar explained the passage differently, he had a right to offer his own interpretation. As Rav Meltzer frequently said about similar situations, "He explains his way, and I explain my way."

Immediately after the lecture, one of the top students ran to the *yeshiva*'s library and looked up the *Sfas Emes*'s commentary. He found that the *Sfas Emes*'s explanation was really consistent with the *Rosh Yeshiva*'s interpretation. The student ran over to Rav Meltzer and told him this. "I am familiar with what the *Sfas Emes* wrote," said Rav Isser Zalman, "and you are right, there is no contradiction there to what I said."

The student was very curious about the *Rosh Yeshiva*'s reaction and walked him home. On the way, Rav Isser Zalman explained, "During the lecture, I noticed a businessman who never before came to my lectures. Also, this fellow who asked the question usually does not ask questions during the lecture. I assumed that there might be a possible *shidduch* (marriage match) between the young man and the businessman's daughter. I'm not certain that this man has a daughter, but most likely he does. Probably the fellow asked the question to impress the businessman that he knows how to learn. I replied the way I did to raise this student in the eyes of his prospective father-in-law."

A few weeks later, the young man who had asked the question actually became engaged to that businessman's daughter.[ז]

જ⁂ૐ

ולא יהיה כקרח וכעדתו
'And he should not be like Korach and like his assembly'
(Bamidbar 17:5)

During the later years of the **Chofetz Chaim** *zt"l*, a big dispute broke out in the Yeshiva of Radin, where he was unofficially the *Rosh Yeshiva*. One day, in middle of *Seder* (learning session) the holy sage entered the *Beis Midrash*. His face was crimson red and his whole body was shaking. He banged on the *bimah* and raised his voice passionately, "Yeshivas Radin was set up on peace. *Machlokes* (strife) has no place here and it should run away from here at once!"

HaRav Mordechai Zukerman *zt"l*, who was a *bochur* in the *yeshiva* at the time, relates that he noticed and felt how deeply distressed the *Chofetz Chaim* was. From that moment on, it made him resent any sort of *machlokes* for the rest of his life -- and he lived to a ripe old age of over 90![ח]

פרשת חקת

Parshas Chukas

זאת חקת התורה
'This is the Decree of the Torah'
(Bamidbar 19:2)

The fact that the Torah uses the language that it does, says **HaRav Moshe Feinstein** *zt"l*, implies that this Decree -- the *Parah Adumah* -- is a Decree that encompasses the entire Torah. It is 'the Decree of the Torah.' But the question is; in what way is it?

Explains Rav Moshe *zt"l*; the wording of the verse teaches us that the entire Torah is actually similar in a certain way to the *Parah Adumah*. As we know, the ashes of the *Parah Adumah* purify those who are ritually impure by contact with a human corpse, and yet, the one who burns the specified parts of the cow, and a pure person who touches or carries the ashes get a slight degree of ritual impurity - מטהר טמאים ומטמא טהורים -. It is like two sides of a coin.

So too, in our lives, every *middah* (character trait), we must utilize to keep Hashem's *Mitzvos*; but on the other hand, it is also possible to, *Chas v'Shalom*, use them for bad things. A very good example of this are the traits of *anavah*, humility, and *gaavah*, haughtiness. A person must use the trait of humility with themselves, meaning to always be humble, and not very exacting about their own honor; but as for the trait of *gaavah*, they must utilize it for their fellow people, and be uncompromising about their honor. For another example, think of the traits of generosity and of stinginess. We must be generous in our giving of charity and *maaser*, but when it comes to the money of our fellow, we should be very tight-fisted, meaning, making sure not to take any money -- not even a penny -- belonging to our fellow, unjustly.

But if, *Chas v'Shalom*, we flip these *middos* around, and use them in the opposite way, then we will be transgressing the Will of Hashem with both of them.א

HaRav Shlomo Ganzfried *zt"l* asks very similarly; why does the Torah say *'This is the Decree of the Torah'*, when, seemingly, it is only the Decree of the *Parah Admuah*?

And he elucidates the matter based on the words of **HaRav Tzvi Heller** *zt"l* in his *sefer Tiv Gittin* on **Midrash Rabbah** 19:3:[38] We Jews must keep the *Mitzvos* of the

---

[38] See there for what he says.

Torah because HaKadosh Baruch Hu said to -- not because of reasons we find for them. And this is what we learn from the wording *'This is the Decree of the Torah'* regarding the *Parah Adumah*: Just like the *Parah Adumah*, which is completely impossible to understand the reason behind with our human intellect, so too, even the *Mitzvos* which we think we know the reasons behind, we should keep like *Chukim*, Commandments which we, as humans cannot understand, and do them only because Hashem commanded us to.[2]

∾

In another explanation, but in the same vein as Rav Moshe *zt"l*'s, the **Trisker Maggid zt"l** says that the Torah is just like the *Parah Adumah* in the aspect that it can be

מטהר טמאים ומטמא טהורים (see above).

How so? That if somebody -- even if they are very lowly -- studies Torah, the Torah purifies them! However, if someone then thinks of themselves as high up, and pure and holy since they studied Torah, then in effect, their study makes them impure. . .[3]

❋ ❋ ❋ ❋ ❋ ❋ ❋ ❋ ❋ ❋ ❋ ❋ ❋

הנגע במת לכל נפש אדם וטמא שבעת ימים. הוא
יתחטא בו ביום השלישי וביום השביעי יטהר ואם לא
יתחטא ביום השלישי וביום השביעי לא יטהר
'One who touches the corpse of any human soul, and he will be impure for seven days. He shall purify

himself with it [the ashes of the Parah Adumah mixed in spring water] on the third day and on the seventh day, [and] be pure; and if he will not purify himself on the third day and on the seventh day, he will not be pure.'
(Bamidbar 19:11-12)

The Torah teaches us here a fundamental lesson: If one wishes to improve -- to purify themselves, they must put in effort to do so. It will not happen if they do not. And if, indeed, a person does put in the necessary effort to improve, then HaKadosh Baruch Hu Himself will help them to.

זאת התורה אדם כי ימות באהל
'This is the Law; if a person will die in a tent. . .'
(Bamidbar 19:14)

Our Sages derive from this verse that *'Words of Torah will not endure except in one who kills himself over them.'*[39] What does this seemingly difficult statement mean? Our *Gedolim* give various wonderful explanations. Below are just a few of them!

Based on a parable,[40] the **Chofetz Chaim** *zt"l* explains that if one is dead, it goes without saying that they are not able to go engage in some other activity. So too with Torah

---

[39] *Berachos* 63b.

[40] See there in ***Chofetz Chaim al HaTorah*** for his wonderful parable!

study, when one is learning, they must totally involve themselves in the Torah, and certainly not become distracted with anything else, as if they are completely unable to.ᵗ

The **Chazon Ish** *zt"l* says that every person is made up of lots of *middos*. Some are good, but others are very bad. If we eliminate and overcome those negative *middos* from ourselves, we are, in effect, killing a part of ourselves -- but this "death" actually confers true, quality life on the person, and words of Torah will endure in them.ⁿ

The *Nikolsburger Rebbe*, **HaRav Yosef Yechiel Michel Lebovits** *shlit"a* elucidates the matter like this: The truth of the matter is that everyone can learn Torah. However, if a person truly wants to internalize the Torah's words, if he wants the Torah he learned to stay with him throughout his life so that he should be a true Torah-person, then he must put "himself" aside. This means that a person who is busy pursuing physical pleasures cannot keep the Torah within himself. He may be learning Torah, but he cannot "keep" it -- he cannot internalize it. Only if a person tries to eliminate and overcome their personal physical desires and quiet their body's appetite for more and more pleasure, only such a person can properly keep the Torah within themselves.ᴵ

Somewhat similarly, the **Maggid of Kozhnitz** *zt"l* says that it means to say that a person must kill the "himself" -- the ego -- within them. We must come to realize that the reason we can do things, or understand Torah, is not from our own power, but from the fact that HaKadosh Baruch Hu gives us strength, and understanding, etc.ᵀ

In response to my question of what the meaning of this *Gemara* is, **HaRav Shmuel Kamenetzky** *shlit"a* explained that we must have self-sacrifice for Torah.[41]

And **HaRav Shimon Schwab** *zt"l* expounds that only if a person kills the "himself" within them -- meaning that he does not learn only for "himself", but also shares his knowledge and teaches Torah to others, then Torah will endure in him.ⁿ

זאת התורה אדם כי ימות באהל כל הבא אל האהל וכל אשר באהל יטמא שבעת ימים. וכל כלי פתוח אשר אין צמיד פתיל עליו טמא הוא

---

41 See **Mishneh Torah**, *Hilchos Talmud Torah*, 3:12.

'This is the Law: If a person will die in a tent, all who come into the tent, and all that is in the tent will be impure for seven days. And every open vessel that no lid is fastened upon it, it is impure.'
(Bamidbar 19:14-15)

In the plain sense, the Torah speaks here of the rules of *Tumas Ohel* -- ritual impurity that comes from being under the same roof-space as a human corpse. And the verse is teaching us that an earthenware vessel, which has special laws with regards to *tumah* (ritual impurity) in the fact that it can only become impure if *tumah* enters into its interior, as we are taught, becomes ritually impure if it doesn't have a lid fastened onto it and it is under the same roof as a human corpse. So **Rashi** *zt"l* brings from *Sifri* here.

But explains the **Maggid of Kozhnitz** *zt"l* homiletically: The *passuk* teaches us that one who speaks however they want, and doesn't guard their tongue from speaking slander or bad words -- they leave their mouths as a vessel without a fastened-on lid -- they are surely 'impure', because they say forbidden things.ע

❋ ❋ ❋ ❋ ❋ ❋ ❋ ❋ ❋ ❋ ❋ ❋ ❋

וירם משה את ידו ויך את הסלע
'And Moshe raised his hand, and he struck the rock'
(Bamidbar 20:11)

In the middle of this *Parsha*, we read about the famous account of HaKadosh Baruch Hu telling Moshe Rabbeinu to speak to a certain rock and it would give water for the *Bnei Yisroel*. But due to certain things, Moshe Rabbeinu struck the rock instead, and, although Hashem still caused it to give forth water, Moshe didn't do what he was supposed to, and he was punished for it by not being able to enter *Eretz Yisroel*. The commentators grapple with what exactly his sin was, and one would do well to see their holy suggestions.

HaRav Moshe Feinstein *zt"l* brings out a beautiful lesson within the command to speak to the rock: It comes to teach us that we need to speak words of Torah and *Mussar* even to those who don't understand -- like a rock, for they will come to understand from all the learning. And a person should not despair of educating their children because they seem like they don't understand, but rather, they should say things over to them until they <u>come</u> to understand.'

❁ ❁ ❁ ❁ ❁ ❁ ❁ ❁ ❁ ❁ ❁ ❁ ❁

ויאמר אליו אדום לא תעבור בי פן בחרב אצא לקראתך

'And Edom said to him, "You shall not pass through me, lest I will go out towards you with the sword!"'
(Bamidbar 20:18)

The Torah uses the word "פן" which is an expression of a possibility, but not a definite. Why did Edom -- the big sword carrier of Esav -- only threaten that "maybe" they would step out with a sword? He surely was happy to do it, so why the doubt?

The *Imrei Binah* writes that Yitzchok blessed Esav " **על חרבך תחיה**" that he would live by his sword, killing people, including Yaakov. Nevertheless, he was only allowed to harm Yaakov if Yaakov did not learn and keep *Mitzvos.* **הקול קול יעקב והידים ידי עשו**. Only when there was no 'Kol Yaakov' (voice of Yaakov) in the *shuls* was Esav able to use his sword on us. Otherwise, he was unable to harm us. It was for this reason that Edom used an expression of uncertainty. Only if *Klal Yisroel* would not behave according to how they were supposed to, will Esav have an ability to use his sword on us.[3]

והיה כל הנשוך וראה אתו וחי

'And it will be that anyone who was bitten, and he will see it [the copper serpent] and live.'
(Bamidbar 21:8)

Since Hashem said this, explains **HaRav Meir Simcha HaKohen of Dvinsk** *zt"l*, then even if someone was sick with some regular illness, and they were close to dying, if they were bitten by one of the snakes, and so they would look at the copper serpent, they would be healed also from the illness they had before, and would return to good health!

Therefore, Rav Meir Simcha continues, a person in such a situation would be happy if one of the snakes bit him, since they would then be able to be healed from their current illness also. And so, the verse uses the word והיה, which, as **Chazal** tell us, is a language of joy.'

וידבר העם באלוקים ובמשה למה העליתנו ממצרים למות במדבר כי אין לחם ואין מים ונפשנו קצה בלחם הקלקל. וישלח השם בעם את הנחשים השרפים וינשכו את העם וימת עם רב מישראל
ויבא העם אל משה ויאמרו חטאנו כי דברנו בהשם ובך התפלל אל השם ויסר מעלינו את הנחש ויתפלל משה בעד העם. ויאמר השם אל משה: עשה לך שרף ושים אתו על נס והיה כל הנשוך וראה אתו וחי ויעש משה נחש נחשת וישמהו על הנס והיה אם נשך הנחש את איש והביט אל נחש הנחשת וחי

'And the people spoke against G-d and against Moshe; "Why have you brought us up from Egypt, to die in the Wilderness. . ." And Hashem sent in the people the fiery serpents, and they bit the people, and a multitude of people from Yisroel died. And the people came to Moshe, and they said "We have sinned, for we have spoken against Hashem, and against you; pray to Hashem, and He should remove the snake from upon us;" and Moshe prayed on behalf of the people. And Hashem said to Moshe; "Make for yourself a fiery [serpent], and place it upon a pole, and it will be that anyone who was bitten, and he will see it and live." And Moshe made a copper serpent, and he placed it upon the pole,

**and it was, if a snake bit a man, and he would gaze
at the copper serpent, and live.'
(Bamidbar 21:5-9)**

Why, asks the **Chofetz Chaim** *zt"l*, when Moshe Rabbeinu *davened* that Hashem remove the frogs in Egypt,[42] his prayer was answered, but when he *davened* that He take away the fiery serpents, his prayer was not entirely effective?

Explains the *Chofetz Chaim*; the *Bnei Yisroel* were punished here for the sin of *lashon hara*, as they spoke against Hashem and Moshe Rabbeinu. Now, it is known that when a person does a sin, it makes a prosecuting angel. This angel doesn't need to necessarily prosecute explicitly, but just its very existence is its prosecution. When a person comes up to Heaven for their judgement, this angel appears on the scene, and its very appearance is testimony enough to the *aveirah*.

However, with the sin of *lashon hara*, the prosecuting angel made through it can and does speak, because it came into being through speech. And it speaks against the person, and explicitly announces about the *aveirah*.

We see that the people's request for Moshe Rabbeinu's prayer that Hashem remove the snakes was in the singular, 'the snake', alluding to the prosecuting angel made by speaking *lashon hara* (see **Arachin** 15b), because once the prosecuting angel would be taken away, then

---

[42] See Shemos 8:4-10.

automatically, the snakes would also be. And so did Moshe pray.

But to this Hashem answered Moshe, that the prosecuting angel made by the *lashon hara* -- one that speaks -- is impossible to remove, because it actually demands in speech that the person who did the sin be punished. So what to do? Hashem said that He would give Moshe Rabbeinu a piece of advice on how to save the Jews from the biting snakes. *"Make for yourself a fiery [serpent]"* and everyone who had been bitten would look at it and live, and not die. What was the significance of this copper serpent? The *Gemara*[43] explains: 'Does a snake put to death or make live? Rather, the main thing was that they would look upwards [at the copper serpent which was placed high on a pole] and subjugate their hearts to their Father in Heaven.' Nothing bad comes from Him. And once they realized this, which would, in essence, be a correction for their earlier complaints and accusations, then they could be healed.ח

וַיֵּצֵא עוֹג מֶלֶךְ הַבָּשָׁן לִקְרָאתָם הוּא וְכָל עַמּוֹ לַמִּלְחָמָה
אֶדְרֶעִי. וַיֹּאמֶר הַשֵּׁם אֶל מֹשֶׁה אַל תִּירָא אֹתוֹ
'And Og, king of the Bashan, went out towards them
-- he and all his people -- to war at Edre'i. And
Hashem said to Moshe, "Do not fear him. . ."'
(Bamidbar 21:33-34)

---

[43] *Rosh Hashanah* 29a.

Why would Moshe Rabbeinu have been afraid of Og? Surely he wasn't worried about his tremendous size, as certainly he trusted fully that Hashem could easily protect them from him. **Rashi** *zt"l* brings from the *Midrash*[44] that Moshe was afraid to wage war on him, because he thought that perhaps he would have great merit from helping Avraham Avinu, as we know that a "refugee" came and told Avraham that Lot was captured -- and that refugee was Og.

Asks *Mori v'Rebbi*, **HaRav Elyakim Rosenblatt** *zt"l*, adapted from a *shmuess* of **HaRav Leib Chasman** *zt"l*, how could Moshe have been afraid of this merit? We learn that Og's intentions in reporting Lot's capture were very lowly![45] So, what merit was there in it, if any at all?!

But we see from here, says *Rabbeinu zt"l*, the incredible power of even a marginal act of kindness, one devoid of all authenticity. Since it was this act of kindness to Avraham which ultimately brought about Lot's rescue, it still retained incredible potency. And if this is so, how many times more precious and powerful is any *Mitzvah* we perform with the proper intent!

❧Maasim Tovim❧

---

[44] *Bamidbar Rabbah; Tanchuma.*

[45] See **Rashi** *zt"l* to Bereishis 14:13.

ויקחו אליך פרה
'And they shall take to you a cow'
(Bamidbar 19:2)

As a young married man, **Rebbe Uri Strelisker** *zt"l* would learn in the *Beis Midrash* in the city of Lemburg, but he was very, very poor.

A very wealthy man of that city saw that Rav Uri was sitting and learning, and he saw that he was really special, so he came to him, and he asked him who he was, etc. and if he had a livelihood. Rav Uri replied to this question, "*Ich hob tzvei kee'in,*" -- "I have two cows," as in *Yiddish*, a *kee* means a cow.

Now, it is a very big and important thing to support Torah scholars. And the rich man went home, and he told his wife to go to Rav Uri Strelisker's house, to his wife, and buy milk from them, in order to give them a means of income.

So, the next day, the rich man's wife went to the *Strelisker's Rebbetzin*, and told her that she wanted to buy milk from her -- "I hear you have cows," she said. But the *Rebbetzin* replied that she didn't know what she (the rich man's wife) was talking about; they didn't have anything like that.

The woman went back to her husband, and told him about what the *Rebbetzin* had said. So, he returned to Rav Uri, and he asked him why he didn't tell him the truth; he had said that he had cows -- *kee'in*!

The *Strelisker* explained that what he meant by *kee'in* was that his livelihood comes from the two words כי in the verse (*Tehillim* 33:21), '**Kee vo yismach libeinu, kee v'Sheim kadsho vatachnu'** -- 'For in Him our heart will rejoice, for in His Holy Name we have trusted.'

Those two *kee's, kee'in,* were the livelihood of **Rebbe Uri Strelisker** *zt"l!*ב

⪻⪼

**וראו כל העדה כי גוע אהרן ויבכו את אהרן שלשים יום
כל בית ישראל**
**'And the entire assembly saw that Aharon had
expired, and the entire house of Israel mourned for
Aharon thirty days.'**
(Bamidbar 20:29)

*Because Aharon pursued peace, and put love between the two
sides of a quarrel and between man and wife (**Rashi zt"l** from
Chazal)*

*Hillel said: Be from the students of Aharon, loving peace, and
pursuing peace, loving the creations, and bringing them closer to
the Torah (**Avos** 1:11)*

When *Mori v'Rebbi*, **HaRav Elyakim Rosenblatt** *zt"l* lived in Briarwood, NY, there was a non-religious woman who passed by their house with her six children around 2:00 AM. *Rabbeinu* was awake, as he was often up very early learning, and he opened the door and invited them to come in.

Now, this made a huge impression on the woman. Because he didn't even know who she, or her children were. Theoretically, they could have been thieves! But he still cordially invited them inside.

The *Rav* spoke to them, and invited them to his *shul*, even though at the time they really hardly knew anything about *frumkeit*.

Although then, her children had married outside the faith, today, her, and all of them are *frum*, in the merit of the *Rav* zt"l, and she has 31 grandchildren who are all *frum* as well!ס

פרשת בלק

Parshas Balak

Writes **HaRav Dovid Nussbaum** *shlit"a*: The *Parsha* tells us that the king of Moav, Balak, hired Bilaam, the famous sorcerer [and prophet], to place a curse upon the Jewish People who were encamped near their border. After accepting the job, Bilaam mounted his donkey intending to ride it to Moav, when the donkey saw an angel blocking its path and veered off the road. Bilaam struck the donkey and the donkey spoke to Bilaam, reprimanding him for striking her. . .

The **Maharal of Prague** *zt"l* contrasts Avraham's saddling and preparing his donkey before departing for Mount Moriah to sacrifice his beloved son, Yitzchok, and Bilaam's saddling his donkey before departing to join king Balak in his war against the Jews. The *Maharal* writes that the word for donkey in Hebrew, *chamor*, denotes the physicality of this world. *Chamor* uses the same letters as the word *chomer*, meaning material physical being. Avraham rode on top of his donkey, meaning that he had elevated his position so that his spiritual status was above the mundane activities of This World. However, the *Maharal* notes that the language employed in conjunction with Bilaam's donkey shows that Bilaam did not ennoble his life with dedication to Hashem's will, although he was a prophet entitled to speak with Hashem.

Life is full of opportunities with which to serve Hashem. Our skills, talents, intellect, persuasive powers and other capabilities are often misused and wasted on non-productive projects. We forget that the spiritual being within us yearns to come closer to Hashem, and, instead, we gravitate towards the normal everyday aspects of life. Speech is a gift from Hashem found only in man. It separates man from the rest of the animal kingdom and indicates that we have a higher calling to attend to.

Bilaam chose to use his ability to speak to curse Hashem's Chosen People. Hashem conveyed, through the donkey berating Bilaam, that Bilaam misused his ability to communicate. Bilaam should have understood this and not [sought to] use cursing the Jews to further his ambition for fame and fortune. However, as **HaRav Moshe Feinstein** *zt"l* comments, Bilaam's hatred for the Jewish People was so great that he was unable to think clearly. Bilaam's donkey was granted the power speech to show Bilaam that absolutely nothing separated him from the level of his donkey. If Bilaam had understood the moral lesson being taught him, he would have returned from his mission immediately after the incident with the donkey.

Hashem leaves us little notes with which to contemplate our behavior and the use of our abilities. Are we paying attention or are we ignoring them like Bilaam and, possibly, leading lives that lead to spiritual oblivion?א

וישלח מלאכים אל בלעם בן בעור . . . לקרא לו לאמר הנה עם יצא ממצרים הנה כסה את עין הארץ . . . הנה העם היצא ממצרים ויכס את עין הארץ

'And he [Balak] sent messengers to Bilaam son of Be'or. . . to summon him, saying: "Behold, a people who went out from Egypt, behold, it covered the eye of the land. . . And Bilaam said. . . "Behold, the people who are going out from Egypt, and it covered the eye of the land"'
(Bamidbar 22:5, 10-11)

The question is asked: Why did Balak speak in the past tense, of a nation who 'went out' of Egypt, while Bilaam spoke in the present tense -- *'who are going out from Egypt'*?

HaRav Shlomo Ganzfried *zt"l* points us to later in this *Parsha*, where we find that Bilaam again speaks about the *Yetzias Mitzraim* in the present tense. He said *'G-d brings them out from Egypt'*. And **Rashi** *zt"l* there explains Bilaam's statement to contrast Balak's: "You said," says Bilaam, *"'Behold, a people who went out from Egypt'* -- but they did not leave Egypt by themselves, rather, Hashem brought them out."

There were non-Jews, explains Rav Ganzfried, who were saying that even though Hashem brought the Jews out of

Egypt, this was only because of His hatred for Egypt, and not from His love of the Jews. And therefore, when they were in the Wilderness, He removed His direct supervision and love for them. But the truth is that even when we went in the Wilderness, HaKadosh Baruch Hu showed us His love with the great miracles that He did for us. And so, our entire journey in the Wilderness, could actually be categorized as part of *Yetzias Mitzraim*.

This is what Bilaam said: '*G-d brings them out from Egypt*' -- meaning: Not only did we not leave Egypt by ourselves, rather <u>He took us</u> out; but further yet, also now, He was "bringing us out" and leading us, and still, His supervision and love was upon us. And this, therefore, explains the different languages used by both Bilaam and Balak. Balak looked at *Yetzias Mitzraim* as a thing of the past, while Bilaam knew that it was still going.[2]

⊰❧⊱

HaRav Moshe Feinstein *zt"l* explains in another vein: One might think that *Klal Yisroel* is just like other nations, who wish to forget their unsavory past before they became a nation and kingdom, but Bilaam knew otherwise: We will always know that we went out of Egypt, and, in fact, we are obligated to remember/mention the *Yetzias Mitzraim* daily. This is one of the qualities of the Jewish People, through which it is possible for us to influence the entire world. And this is what Bilaam was afraid of. But if it was as Balak thought, that we are like all other nations, and we wish to just forget our past -- that we were strangers in Egypt, and that Hashem took us out from there -- then there wouldn't have been what to fear, because we would have just mixed with the rest of the peoples. Therefore, Balak said that we covered the eye of the land, in the past tense, but Bilaam said ויכס, which can also mean in the future tense.[1]

⚜

Somewhat similarly to the above insights, **HaRav Eliyahu Schlesinger** *shlit"a* elucidates that Balak's perspective of the emerging Jewish nation was quite different than that of Bilaam. Balak viewed *Klal Yisroel* through his human eyes, which gave him only a superficial view of the nation. He saw the "here and now" of the Jewish People. Bilaam, however, as a prophet who related what Hashem told him, could speak only the absolute truth. Thus, his perspective was quite different.

Balak was aware that the Jews were privy to an array of exceptional and unprecedented miracles and wonders as they left Egypt. Balak figured that it was all over -- the miracles and their influence were in the past. After all, let us look at the history of the Jews during their sojourn in the Wilderness. They complained bitterly when they did not receive meat. When water was at a premium, they complained. The *meraglim*, episode of the spies, caused a big *Chilul Hashem*, desecration of Hashem's Name. Is it any wonder that Balak felt that this nation had <u>left</u> Egypt? They seemed to have severed any relationship with the past. A people that has broken its ties with the past has little foundation upon which to build its future. They should be easy to curse effectively, because, seemingly, they had already handicapped themselves by dissociating themselves from the Al-mighty.

Bilaam, on the other hand, was an individual in whom Hashem placed His Words. Thus, he could articulate only the truth. He saw a nation that was <u>leaving</u> Egypt. It was not an event that had passed, but rather, it was an ongoing manifestation of Hashem's miraculous power and awesome might. This nation had neither severed its bond with the Almighty nor disconnected itself from the Egyptain Exodus. It is an experience that is alive and well in their minds and hearts, continuing to inspire them. Veritably, they had had setbacks, but these were merely delays that had temporarily impeded their march towards their home in *Eretz Yisroel*. Yes, their past is linked with their present.ז

❋ ❋ ❋ ❋ ❋ ❋ ❋ ❋ ❋ ❋ ❋ ❋ ❋ ❋

This whole episode with Bilaam, says **HaRav Moshe Feinstein** *zt"l*, comes to teach us a big lesson: Even though Bilaam, being a prophet, knew that Hashem didn't want him to curse *Klal Yisroel*, nevertheless, he still tried to do this big sin. We learn from here that we must be very careful, and we mustn't rely only on our wisdom, etc. because we are liable to still, *Chas v'Shalom*, fall into the trap if the *Yetzer Hara* if we aren't extremely careful.ח

❋ ❋ ❋ ❋ ❋ ❋ ❋ ❋ ❋ ❋ ❋ ❋ ❋ ❋

**ויען בלעם ויאמר אל עבדי בלק אם יתן לי בלק מלא
ביתו כסף וזהב לא אוכל לעבר את פי השם**
*'And Bilaam answered, and he said to the servants of
Balak: "If Balak were to give me his houseful of silver
and gold, I would not be able to transgress the word
of Hashem. . ."'*
(Bamidbar 22:18)

We find, notes **HaRav Yaakov Kamenetzky** *zt"l*, a similar, yet different, language used in the *Mishnah* (*Avos* 6:9), where Rav Yose ben Kisma says that even if he were to be given <u>all</u> the silver, gold, and precious stones, he still would only dwell in a place of Torah.

The difference between them is that Bilaam made a limit to his statement -- '*his houseful*'. If Balak would have given him two housefuls, or more, of silver, gold, etc. then he <u>would</u> have transgressed Hashem's Word. But Rav Yose ben Kisma spoke of all the riches and valuables in the entire world -- even if he would be offered all of them to live not in a place of Torah, he wouldn't accept.[1]

❊ ❊ ❊ ❊ ❊ ❊ ❊ ❊ ❊ ❊ ❊ ❊ ❊

**ויאמר אלקים אל בלעם לא תלך עמהם לא תאר את
העם**
*'And G-d said to Bilaam; "You shall not go with them
(עמהם)! You shall not curse the people. . .'*
(Bamidbar 22:12)

**ויבא אלקים אל בלעם לילה ויאמר לו אם לקרא לך באו
האנשים קום לך אתם ואך את הדבר אשר אדבר אליך**

**אתו תעשה ויקם בלעם בבקר ויחבש את אתנו וילך עם
שרי מואב ויחר אף אלקים כי הולך הוא**

*'And G-d came to Bilaam at night, and He said to
him, "If to summon you the men have come, arise,
go with them (אתם), but only the thing that I will
speak to you -- it you shall do. And Bilaam arose in
the morning, and he saddled his donkey, and he went
with (עם) the officers of Moav. And the anger of G-d
burned, because he was going. . .'*
(Bamidbar 22:20-22)

Says the **Vilna Gaon** *zt"l*: All the commentators ask;
since at first Hashem told Bilaam not to go, how
could He have given him permission, as if He "changed
His mind"? And also, since He did give him permission,
why did He get angry with him for going?

Explains the *Gaon* wonderfully: There is a difference (at
least in this context) between the two words used for
'with' -- **עם** and **את**.[46] The word **עם** connotes equalness in
that certain matter. Two (or more) people are doing
something with the same intention. Everything that they
are doing together is with one intention and desire. The
word **עם** does not apply, though, in a case where one
person is only passively part of the action, even if their
intention is still the same.

---

[46] Obviously, I am not learned enough to be able to list all the places in
Tanach where such words are used and explain them according to this,
but if the **Vilna Gaon** says it, then surely it must work!

The word **את**, however, implies that even though people are doing the same thing together, they don't have the same intention, and their heart is not identical in the matter. Or, even though they are both doing the same thing, <u>and</u> with the same intent, nevertheless, one is active in the matter, and the other is just passively involved, then, the root **את** also applies.

At first, elucidates the *Gaon*, Hashem told Bilaam '*You shall not go with them* -- **עמהם**', meaning: Balak's officers' intent was for Bilaam to curse *Klal Yisroel*, and Hashem warned Bilaam to not go with the intention to curse, as well. As He added '*You shall not curse the people*'. Afterwards, when Bilaam really strained to go, then Hashem gave him permission '*to go with them – *אתם', i.e. He had already told him not to go in the category of **עמהם**, with the intent to curse *Bnei Yisroel*, but He was giving permission only for him to go **אתם**, with his heart not being similar to theirs. Now, if Bilaam had done just that, Hashem would not have been angry at him. But Bilaam, in his wickedness, didn't do so; as the *passuk* testifies '*he went with (*עם*) the officers of Moav*', and as **Rashi** *zt"l* quotes from **Chazal** that 'his heart was like their heart, equal.' Meaning that he intended to curse the Jews. Therefore, Hashem got very upset with him, as he had disobeyed His direct command!

Yet we see afterwards that the Angel told him (v. 35) '*Go with (*עם*) the men*'! However, we must look at what **Rashi** says there, that in the way which a person wishes to go, they are led. Bilaam wanted so badly to go with the officers of Moav equally, and curse the Jews, and had tried so hard to so, and now, his portion would end up like theirs, and he would end up getting punishment equal to theirs.'

ויפתח **השם** את פי האתון ותאמר לבלעם מה עשיתי לך
כי הכיתני זה שלש רגלים. ויאמר בלעם לאתון

*'And Hashem opened the mouth of the she-donkey
and she said to Bilaam, "What did I do to you that
you struck me these three times?" And Bilaam said to
the she-donkey. . .'*
(Bamidbar 22:28)

HaRav Gershon Unger *shlit"a* told me the following: A person can be so caught up in his narrow perspective on things that he can miss the obvious. Bilaam did not even realize a miracle was taking place, that his donkey was speaking to him.

And he added that he heard this from **HaRav Avigdor Miller** *zt"l*: "A person can be so oblivious of his own character flaw that he spends his entire life never being aware of that which someone else who meets him for the first time recognizes immediately."

ותראני האתון ותט לפני זה שלש רגלים אולי נטתה
מפני כי עתה גם אתכה הרגתי ואותה החייתי

'And the donkey saw me, and turned before me these three times; if it had not turned from before me. . . I would have killed you, and I would have let it live.'
(Bamidbar 22:33)

Adapted from a *shmuess* of **HaRav Chaim Shmuelevitz** *zt"l*, says *Mori v'Rebbe*, **HaRav Elyakim Rosenblatt** *zt"l*: This section of the *parsha* describes the events following Bilaam's encounter with the Angel when he, Bilaam, was on his way to curse *Klal Yisroel*. The Angel of Hashem, with his sword drawn, stood in Bilaam's path, ready to oppose him. Bilaam did not detect the angel's presence, however the donkey did see the Angel, and detoured from the path. This occurred three times, and each time Bilaam beat his donkey for not continuing on the path. Hashem opened the mouth of the donkey, giving it the power of speech. The donkey rebuked Bilaam, according to **Rashi** *zt"l* from *Midrashim*, saying: "What have I done to you that you beat me these three times? Have I ever been in the habit of doing this to you?" "No," replied Bilaam. Thus Bilaam was reproved by his donkey. He could not answer the rebuke of his donkey to justify his beating her.

Rashi explains the meaning of our *passuk* as follows: The Angel of Hashem said to Bilaam, "Had the donkey not turned aside. . . I would have killed you and spared the donkey. But now that the donkey did detour from its path and you struck it, causing it to rebuke you and you had no answer to its reprimand, I was obligated to kill it. For, if the donkey were to remain alive, Bilaam would have been terribly embarrassed. People who would see this donkey

118

would say, "This is the very donkey whose rebuke reproved Bilaam. Bilaam is the human being who could not answer the rebuke of a mere animal." Thus -- according to *Rashi*, the Angel of Hashem killed the donkey in order to spare the humiliation of Bilaam. Hashem had respect for Bilaam's honor.

We see from here how Heaven evaluates the honor due a human being, even one so vile as Bilaam HaRasha. Hashem deemed it appropriate that the donkey should die, thereby foregoing an opportunity for even a great sanctification of His Name, by its remaining alive. Why? In order to avoid embarrassment for even this most loathsome of individuals. Had the donkey lived, Bilaam would have suffered humiliation whenever people would comment, "This is the donkey whose rebuke reproved Bilaam."

We must realize the significance of the honor that is due to each and every human being, no matter who he or she is. Each individual deserves proper respect by virtue of the fact that he was created in the Divine Image. We must constantly bear this principle in mind and train ourselves to develop our sensitivities to treat each other with dignity and respect.

We must never say or do anything that can bring another individual even the slightest degree of embarrassment. May we be *zoche* to attain this lofty level of *Bein Adam L'chaveiro. Amein.*

ומה אזעם לא זעם השׁם
'And how can I anger, if Hashem has not angered?'
(Bamidbar 23:8)

In a different twist on this translation, we may see a tremendous lesson: Each person must ask themselves this question: *'How can I anger'* -- how can I lose my temper or become angry at someone, *'if Hashem has not angered'* -- if Hashem is so patient with me, and holds back His anger, although I often am deserving of punishment?

כעת יאמר ליעקב ולישראל מה פעל א-ל
'At a time it will be said to Yaakov and to Yisroel, "What has G-d done?"'
(Bamidbar 23:23)

The word מה, says the **Chofetz Chaim** *zt"l*, can be used to express a question, or to connote greatness, as in the phrase *'How abundant is Your good! –* מה רב טובך'.

There are times when people lament and complain, or simply ask the question, "What has Hashem done?" -- i.e. why has He hid His Face from us, letting us be afflicted by cruel people sometimes?

But there will come a day when Hashem will "relent" on His People, and then, it will be made known throughout the entire world *'What has Hashem done'* -- in the form of

120

praise – that even all those times when we felt such questions arise, everything was for our benefit.ⁿ

הן עם כלביא יקום
'Behold, a People who will arise like a lioness'
(Bamidbar 23:24)

Says **Rashi** *zt"l* from *Midrash Tanchuma*: When they arise from their sleep in the morning, they strengthen themselves like a lion to grab *Mitzvos*, to don *Tallis*, to read the *Shema*, and to lay *Tefillin*.

It is very appropriate for us to cite here the opening words of the **Shulchan Aruch** (**Orach Chaim**, *siman* 1, *se'if* 1): '*One should strengthen himself like a lion to arise in the morning to the service of his Creator, that it should be that he awakens the dawn.*'

Kitzur Shulchan Aruch (*siman* 1, *se'if* 2) goes into further detail: And also, while lying upon his bed, a person should know before Whom he lies, and immediately when he awakens from his sleep, he should remember the kindnesses of Hashem, may He be blessed, that He did with him: He returned to him his Soul, which he had entrusted to Him weary, and He returned it to him fresh and relaxed. . . '*They are new for the mornings; abundant is Your faithfulness!*' (*Eichah* 3:23). Meaning that every morning, a person becomes a new creation, and he should give thanks with all his heart to Hashem, may His Name be blessed, for this. And while he is still on his bed, he should say: *"I give thanks before You, living and everlasting King, for You returned in me my Soul with compassion, abundant is Your faithfulness --* **מודה אני לפניך מלך חי וקים** **שהחזרת בי נשמתי בחמלה רבה אמונתך.**

And he continues also in *se'if* 4: A person needs to strengthen himself like a lion, and immediately, when he awakens from his sleep (and says *Modeh Ani*, etc.), he should arise with alacrity to the service of the Creator, may He be blessed and exalted, before the *yetzer hara* overcomes him with arguments and excuses to not arise. . . and he should put as his objective the Will of the King, King of kings, HaKadosh Baruch Hu.

מה טבו אהליך יעקב משכנתיך ישראל
'How good are your tents, Yaakov! Your dwelling places, Yisroel!'
(Bamidbar 24:5)

Why, asks **HaRav Shmuel Yaakov Rubenstein** *zt"l*, was it chosen to begin our morning prayers with these words, which were said by Bilaam?

If you look in **Rashi** *zt"l*, he brings from *Bava Basra* 60a that Bilaam said this blessing because he saw how the Jews' tents were set up in a modest way. The beginning of *Kedusha* (sanctity), explains Rav Rubenstein, is not in the *shuls*, but rather, their *kedusha* flows from the 'opening of the tent', meaning, from the Jewish homes. If **מה טבו** **אהליך יעקב** -- in the house, the sanctity of the Jewish

People is safeguarded, then משכנתיך ישראל -- the *Shechinah* will rest on us. If the "tent" is in the category of 'Yaakov', a proper Jewish home, then the *shuls* will be the Sanctuary of Yisroel.ע

❧❧

Another possible explanation: The name Yisroel, we are taught, can refer to great and high people, like *Gedolim*, and the name Yaakov may be employed in reference to "regular" Jews.[47]

Also, a tent is more of a temporary setting, while a dwelling place connotes a more permanent place. However, they both imply a place of Torah study -- just again, one intimating more temporary and one more permanent. Now let us put this all together:

'*How good are your Tents, Yaakov!*': One might, *Chas v'Shalom* think that if they are "just a regular Jew", and they go to learn Torah only sometimes, the *Beis Midrash* (or any place they learn) being only a temporary dwelling place for them, it is not that good or important.

But the above verse teaches us otherwise: Every single good thing which we do is precious to Hashem; He does not overlook anything. Thus, even if you have to be working most of the day, and then you come home pretty late, and go learn even a little; that is extremely precious

---

[47] See the **Ohr HaChaim HaKadosh** to our verse.

to Hashem! Don't get discouraged and think that your Torah is not important; it is very important! And a proof for this: If you take the *Gematria* (numerical value) of the words 'מה טבו אהליך יעקב' -- '*How good are your tents, Yaakov!*', it equals 310. What does that correspond to? The word 'יש' -- *yeish*, (which means literally 'there is' or 'there are'). 'יש' is the opposite of 'אין' -- *ayin* (nothingness). Meaning that whatever Torah you are able to learn -- it is not nothingness, *Chas v'Shalom*. It is the very opposite. 'There is' much, much importance to it! Furthermore, it alludes to the teaching in the last Mishnah in Uktzin (3:12) that in the future, HaKadosh Baruch Hu will give to Tzaddikim 310 worlds, as the passuk says (Mishlei 8:21), 'להנחיל אהבי יש -- To cause My loved ones to inherit יש (which has the *gematria* of 310).' This brings out even more the tremendous value and importance of it.

And on the other hand, the verse says '*Your Dwelling Places, Yisroel!*': To all people who <u>can</u> and <u>are</u> involved in Torah study etc. most of the day, realize just how good <u>every moment</u> of it is to Hashem, as well!

The **Baal Shem Tov** *zt"l* once said that even when a Jew comes home, exhausted from a hard day's work, and says '*Oy!* It's just a few minutes before sundown,' and quickly prays *Mincha*, the Heavenly Angels tremble from the holiness of that prayer.'

Furthermore, there is yet something else we can see from the above verse: A person is not stuck in one place; the verse implies that you can move up from the category of a 'Yaakov' -- a "regular" person (which as we saw, is very lofty!), into the second category of a *Gadol B'Yisroel*. With hard work and the help of Hashem, of course. And these things are vital to realize early on in our day.

❋❋❋❋❋❋❋❋❋❋❋❋❋❋

◆Maasim Tovim◆

מלא ביתו כסף וזהב
'His house filled with silver and gold'
(Bamidbar 22:18)

Once there was a generous Jew who gave a lot of charity, but yet, was not all that wealthy himself. Hashem blessed him, and he soon became quite rich. But unfortunately, the man now became very stingy and tight-fisted with his money.

There was a *Rebbe* whom this man had a connection with, and he heard about what was going on, and went to see him. The *Rebbe* traveled to where the man lived, and came to his house. After being let in, the *Rebbe* took the wealthy man to the window and asked him what he saw.

"I see children playing; elderly people walking; and people working."

Then the *Rebbe* took a mirror and put it in front of his face. "What do you see now?" he asked. "Myself." the man replied.

The *Rebbe* explained: When one gets so involved in money, it makes them only able to see themselves. It clouds their vision. That is the difference between a mirror and a window -- that a mirror has silver behind it -- and that is why you see completely different sights in both of them.ᵃ

מות ישרים
'The death of the righteous'
(Bamidbar 23:10)

It is related about the *Alter of Kelm*, HaRav Simcha Zissel Ziv *zl"l*, that before his passing, a fan was placed above his head in order to help with the air. His pains increased from moment to moment, and the agony of death began.

With the last bit of life-breath in him, he exerted himself, and very carefully removed with his hands the fan from above his head, so that it would not end up perhaps getting broken.

All those standing near were amazed at the sight of this incredible effort of the dying man, to not ruin even a little thing like this, which was borrowed from a neighbor. Such was the *Alter*'s great holiness and care to not commit even a trace of thievery, until it became his second nature -- even in the last moments, as his Soul departed from him.ᵇ

❋ ❋ ❋ ❋ ❋ ❋ ❋ ❋ ❋ ❋ ❋ ❋ ❋

פרשת פינחס

Parshas Pinchas

In each *Parsha* from *Behaaloscha* to *Balak*, we read about at least one sin committed. In *Behaaloscha*, the *Bnei Yisroel* complain against Hashem, and then Miriam and Aharon are involved in [slight] slander against Moshe Rabbeinu. In *Shelach*, the episode of the *Meraglim*; in *Korach*, it is the sin of Korach and his assembly. *Parshas Chukas* contains the incident of Moshe Rabbeinu striking the rock, instead of speaking to it as Hashem commanded (see there for further explanation on the matter), and in *Balak*, we read how the *Bnei Yisroel* sinned with the daughters of Midian and Moav.

However, once Pinchas came and performed his great act of zealousness for Hashem (see 25:7-8), the chain was broken: No transgression [as far as I have seen] is performed in *Parshas Pinchas*. We see here the incredible power of a good deed and what it can accomplish.

וידבר השם אל משה לאמר פינחס בן אלעזר בן אהרן הכהן השיב את חמתי מעל בני ישראל
'And Hashem spoke to Moshe, saying: "Pinchas son of Elazar son of Aharon HaKohen returned My wrath from upon the Bnei Yisroel. . ."'
(Bamidbar 25:10-11)

Since the Tribes were speaking ill of Pinchas and saying, "Did you see this 'son of Puti', whose mother's father (Yisro), at one point fattened calves for idol worship, and he, Pinchas, killed a prince of a Tribe of Israel?!", therefore, the *passuk* comes and traces his lineage after Aharon. (**Rashi** *zt"l* from **Chazal**).

The *Seforim* explain that the Tribes suspected Pinchas, saying that the reason he killed Zimri was because he had in him some nature of cruelty, being a descendant of Yisro, who, at one time, before his conversion, had been an idol worshipper. Therefore, the *passuk* came and traced his lineage to Aharon HaKohen, who, as we know, was a 'lover of peace and pursuer of peace'[48] in order to prove that really, Pinchas' nature was like Aharon's, and he did what he did only because of pure zealousness for Hashem.א

❧❧

In a similar vein, the **Baalei Mussar** say that one of Aharon's biggest traits was *chesed*, kindness. Therefore, Pinchas was traced back to him, because his zealousness was actually coming from his trait of *chesed*, goodness, and *ahavas Yisroel* (love of Jews), for he turned away the wrath of Hashem from upon Yisroel.ב

The previous *Slonimer Rebbe*, **HaRav Shalom Noach Berezovsky zt"l**, as well, says that Pinchas' deed was one of *chesed*, and he explains that that is why he was rewarded with things related to *chesed* -- Hashem's Covenant of Peace, and of *Kehunah*.[49] He acted with *gevurah*, strength, for the sake of *chesed*. And truly, the inner part of the deed was completely *chesed*.ב

❧❧

In accordance with the opinion of **Reish Lakish**, that Pinchos was Eliyahu HaNavi, there is a beautiful dialogue

---

[48] *Avos* 1:12

[49] See *Zohar* vol. 3, 145b.

recorded in the *Yalkut Shimoni*:[50] HaKadosh Baruch Hu said to him: "You put peace between Israel and between Me in This World; also in the future, you are the one who is destined to put peace between Me and My children." Like it says, *'Behold! I am sending to you Eliyah(u) HaNavi before the coming of the Day of Hashem. . . and he will return the heart of fathers with children.'*

❋ ❋ ❋ ❋ ❋ ❋ ❋ ❋ ❋ ❋ ❋ ❋ ❋

וידבר השם אל משה לאמר צרור את המדינים והכיתם אותם

'And Hashem spoke to Moshe saying: "Trouble the Midianim, and smite them."'
(Bamidbar 25:16-17)

Tells us the **Ohr HaChaim HaKadosh**: Even though the actual battle against the Midianim would take place only later, as we find in *Parshas Mattos*, the command was given now. The intention in this was to bring the Jews to hate the people who had just brought them to sin, and to loath and abominate the seemingly "sweet" and "good" things that came from them. And in this mindset, the Jews would be distanced from the desires which they had acted upon when they sinned with the Midiani and Moavi girls, and these desires would become strange and foreign to them.

❋ ❋ ❋ ❋ ❋ ❋ ❋ ❋ ❋ ❋ ❋ ❋ ❋

---

[50] On the beginning of *Pinchas; remez* 771:18

חנוך משפחת החנכי
'Chanoch, the family of the Chanochi'
(Bamidbar 26:5)

Rashi *zt"l* brings from the *Midrash*: Since the nations were saying that the Egyptians had violated the Jewish mothers in Egypt, and thus our lineage was not pure, Hashem put His Name on each of the family names, giving His own Testimony that this was not so, and every family line came from both Jewish mothers and fathers, and were untainted. He put a ה, *hei*, at the beginning of each name and a י, *yud*, at the end, which are the letters of His Name י-ה. There was one name that was an exception, though -- ימנה, as it already had those letters at the beginning and end of the name itself.

Why, though, asks the **Kli Yakar** *zt"l*, did Hashem not give His Testimony to the purity of our pedigree in the first census?

And he answers that it is because we weren't yet suspected of inappropriate things until we stumbled with the Midiani and Moavi girls. Once we did that, however, it gave the nations room to say that how we behaved then was a sign for how we must have behaved in Egypt. Just like the Jewish males did improper things with the women of Midian and Moav, so too, in Egypt, the Jewish women must have ended up doing improper things, as the Egyptians surely ruled over them.

However, as we saw above, Hashem testified to our cleanliness. All the babies were born from a pure union between **איש**, man, and **אשה**, woman, with the Name **י-ה** between it.

The *Kli Yakar* continues and tells us the significance of the **ה**, *hei*, being at the beginning of each name and the **י**, *yud*, at the end: The *hei* is the woman's part of Hashem's Name **י-ה**, and the *yud* is the man's -- **איש**, **אשה**. The order in which the letters are put is to make known the purity of the Jewish women, since they were, truthfully, more guarded against illicit relations than the men, as we find that the Torah publicizes Shelomis bas Divri,[51] from which we can infer that all the other women were extremely modest, for if not, they too would have been publicized for their wrongdoing. (***Vayikra Rabbah*** 32:5). Therefore, the *hei* is put before the *yud,* because the main thing it was proving was the purity of the Jewish women, that the Egyptians did not "rule over them."

לאזני משפחת האזני
'To Azni, the family of the Azni'
(Bamidbar 26:16)

Rashi *zt"l* says that Ozni is really Etzbon. Many wonder, says the **Shlah HaKadosh**, what is the connection between these two names?

---

[51] See Vayikra 24:11 and **Rashi** there.

Says the *Shlah* that he heard a *mussar*-hint regarding it: **Chazal** say[52] that our fingers were created in a shape like a peg so that we would be able to put them in our ears and stop ourselves from hearing bad things.

The name **אצבון** is similar to the word for finger, **אצבע**, and the name **אזני** is related to the word for ear, **אוזן**!

**אלה בני בנימן למשפחתם ופקדיהם חמשה וארבעים
אלף ושש מאות
אלה בני דן למשפחתם . . . ארבעה וששים אלף וארבע
מאות**

'These are the sons of Binyomin according to their families, and their countings, forty-five thousand and six hundred. These are the sons of Don according to their families. . . sixty-four thousand and four hundred.'
(Bamidbar 26:41-43)

Binyomin, notes the **Chofetz Chaim** *zt"l*, had ten sons, while Don had only one son -- Chushim, and he was deaf. And even so, the Tribe of Don ended up more numerous in population than that of Binyomin!

From this we learn, says Rav Yisroel Meir beautifully, that in whomever Hashem desires,[53] He is able to make them successful from one son more than one who has ten

---

[52] *Kesubos* 5b.

[53] Not to say, of course, that Hashem did *not* desire in Binyomin.

sons. And the same is true with possessions; sometimes a poor person prospers and is happy, while a rich person doesn't so much. Hashem is in control.ה

✿✿✿

Adds **HaRav Avraham Yaakov HaKohen Pam** *zt"l*: In life, one can never predict how things will eventually turn out. At times, the accomplishments of a *ben yachid* (only child) can be more than that of ten children. Even in a large family, the *ben zekunim'l* (child born to parents when they are older) can be the one who eventually brings his parents the most joy and *nachas*.

One cannot give up on a person, no matter what the handicap or disability. It often happens that the one who is considered "least likely to succeed," is the one who produces the greatest achievements. Hashem has endowed every human Soul with immense treasures. Parents of handicapped children should take inspiration and *chizuk* from the accomplishments of Chushim, and realize that they, too, can see great *nachas* from their offspring.ו

ותקרבנה בנות צלפחד בן חפר בן גלעד בן מכיר בן מנשה . . . ותעמדנה לפני משה ולפני אלעזר הכהן ולפני הנשיאם וכל העדה פתח אהל מועד לאמר אבינו מת במדבר והוא לא היה בתוך העדה הנועדים על השם

בעדת קרח כי בחטאו מת ובנים לא היו לו למה יגרע שם
אבינו מתוך משפחתו כי אין לו בן תנה לנו אחזה

*'And the daughters of Tzelafchad son of Cheifer, son
of Gilad, son of Machir, son of Menashe
approached. . . And they stood before Moshe and
before Elazar the Kohen, and before the Princes and
the entire Assembly, at the entrance of the Tent of
Meeting, saying: "Our father died in the Wilderness,
and he was not in the midst of the assembly who
were gathered together against Hashem, in the
assembly of Korach, but for his sin he died, and he
did not have any sons. Why should the name of our
father be diminished from the midst of his family
because he didn't have a son? Give to us an
inheritance. . ."'*
(Bamidbar 27:1-4)

The *Gemara*[54] teaches us that someone who is 'killed by the king' – **הרוגי מלכות** -- their possessions go to the king. **Rashi** *zt"l* explains that this can refer to someone who was to be put to death because they rebelled against one the Jewish kings (see *Sefer Yehoshua* ch. 1).

Suggests **HaRav Meir Simcha HaKohen of Dvinsk** *zt"l*, it is possible that since the daughters of Tzelafchad were very learned, they therefore knew the above law. And, being that Moshe Rabbeinu had the status a king (see Devarim 33:5), the **עדת קרח** could fall under the category of **הרוגי מלכות**, as their main rebellion was against him, and if Tzelafchad had been part of it, his inheritance

---

[54] *Sanhedrin 48b*

would have gone to Moshe.[55] Therefore, these wise women emphasized that Tzelafchad was <u>not</u> part of the assembly of Korach, but rather died for his own sin -- a sin of the kind that his possessions would still have gone to his heirs, and therefore, they rightfully could come with the request that they did. (See *Sanhedrin* ibid. and *Rashi* to v. 3.)ᵀ

קח לך את יהושע בן נון איש אשר רוח בו
'Take Yehoshua son of Nun, a man in whom there is spirit'
(Bamidbar 27:18)

Moshe Rabbeinu asked Hashem to appoint someone over the Congregation. Hashem's choice as the future leader of *Klal Yisroel* was Yehoshua, a man in whom, as the above *passuk* says, *'there is spirit'*.

The question is, says the **Alter of Novhardok** *zt"l*, would we even think that someone without 'spirit in them' would be chosen as leader? So then what does this phrase come to teach us?

The meaning of *'a man in whom there is spirit'*, says the *Alter*, is a man who rules over his <u>own</u> spirit; a person who leads

---

[55] Although Moshe was from the Tribe of Levi, which didn't receive a portion in the Land, he might have just given it, in his generosity, to someone else, as Rav Meir Simcha explains.

all their strengths in accordance with the Will of Hashem. Such a person is also able to lead a nation.ⁿ

* * * * * * * * * * * * * *

וסמכת את ידך עליו
'And you shall lean your hand upon him'
(Bamidbar 27:18)

The *Midrash* (*Bamidbar Rabbah* 21:15) says on this, that it was like lighting a candle from another candle.

The **Netziv, HaRav Naftali Tzvi Yehuda Berlin** *zt"l*, elucidates this comparison: As we know, when you use one candle to light another one, this does not detract from the flame of the first. So too, when Moshe Rabbeinu conferred strength onto Yehoshua, it did not detract from himself at all, rather, it was like 'lighting a candle from another candle.'ᵗ

* * * * * * * * * * * * * *

וביום השבת שני כבשים בני שנה תמימם
'And on the Shabbos day, two sheep in their first year, perfect.'
(Bamidbar 28:9)

The *Gemara*[56] tells us that everybody agrees that these two sheep must be equal to each other in certain ways.

What is the significance of this? Explains **HaRav Moshe Feinstein** *zt"l*; these two sheep correspond to the two aspects of Shabbos -- *Zachor* and *Shamor*, which Hashem said in one utterance, as **Chazal** tell us. *Zachor* is the aspect of remembering the Shabbos, and to make sure we enjoy the Shabbos, such as by eating nicer food, etc. While *Shamor* is the negative commandment to not perform any of the forbidden labors on the Shabbos.

And the fact that these two sheep must be practically identical teaches us that both aspects of Shabbos, both *Shamor* and *Zachor*, must be kept on the same level as each other. For, one who only, or mainly, focuses on the aspect of refraining from doing forbidden *melachos* on the Shabbos, as if it is just a day of restriction, the Shabbos becomes a sort of test for them, as they feel like they are losing out because they can't work today. And, while it is possible that they themselves will stand strong, overcome their *yetzer hara*, and still keep the Shabbos -- albeit unhappily -- it is very likely that their children will end up not keeping the Shabbos when they grow up, as they see only the pain that their parents went through to keep the Shabbos, but no positive side to it. No joy in it.

But in truth, aside from the aspect of *Shamor*, we were also given the aspect of *Zachor*, that is, that we should make

---

[56] *Yoma* 62b

138

sure to enjoy the beautiful Shabbos, and take delight in it. And we must realize that not only are we not losing anything by keeping the Shabbos, as when Hashem set up how people would earn their livelihood, He set it up in a way that one doesn't need to work on the Shabbos, but better even, all types of bountiful blessings come from keeping Shabbos![57] And even if it ever seems to us, in our flawed perspective, that we lost money from keeping the Shabbos, it would all be more than worth it, anyway! Just like we aren't upset to spend a little bit of money to buy something very nice, and we in fact are happy to, so too, with the Shabbos! And if one keeps the Shabbos this way, with both *Shamor* <u>and</u> *Zachor*, more likely than not, their children will want to continue the holy heritage, as they see the tremendous joy in keeping the Shabbos.

This, explains Rav Moshe beautifully, is the significance of the two sheep having to be equal, and of why the two aspects of *Zachor* and *Shamor* were said in one utterance. Because we must fulfill both aspects equally.'

✻ ✻ ✻ ✻ ✻ ✻ ✻ ✻ ✻ ✻ ✻ ✻ ✻

There are 168 *pessukim* in *Parshas Pinchas*, making it the second longest *parsha* in the Torah.

The number 168 corresponds to the *gematria* (numerical value) of the words בעיני השם (if you spell out the Four Letter Name). This alludes to Pinchas' deed and part of the greatness of it: Although he might not have been the

---

⁵⁷ See *Zohar* vol. 2, 62.

139

most popular amongst people for what he did (see **Rashi** *zt"l* to 26:5, quoted above), he thought primarily about what was proper in Hashem's eyes, and he acted accordingly.

&Maasim Tovim&

תחת אשר קנא לאלקיו
'Because he was zealous for his G-d'
(Bamidbar 25:13)

HaRav Yechezkel Abramsky *zt"l* once walked into the *yeshiva* which he taught in, and he said to the *bochurim*: "You are probably very proud that you *davened* Mincha. You probably feel like Hashem "owes you one", as it were. But let me tell you that I just came from the hospital and there are many patients who would love to <u>be able</u> to *daven Mincha*! You must realize: You had the merit to do *Mincha*! It's a privilege -- you are fortunate!"א'

שאו את ראש כל עדת בני ישראל
'Take a count [lit. lift up the heads] of the entire
Assembly of the Children of Israel'
(Bamidbar 26:2)

One morning, the *Chassidim* of the **Chozeh of Lublin** *zt"l* noticed that during *Shacharis*, he skipped the *beracha* of *Shelo asani goy* -- the blessing thanking Hashem for making us a Jew. They were quite curious about this, and after *davening*, the *Rebbe* explained:

He had woken up kind of sad that morning. And he had been very upset, until he saw a non-Jew walking by outside. He reflected on how they begin their day and generally go and engage in nothingness, while we get up to perform our *Avodas Hashem*! The *Rebbe* became so thankful just to be a Jew that he said the *beracha* of *Shelo asani goy* right then and there! And that is why he didn't say it in the *berachos* of *Shacharis*.ⁿ

פרשת מטות

Parshas Mattos

לא יחל דברו ככל היצא מפיו יעשה
*'He shall not desecrate his word; like all that goes
out of his mouth, he shall do.'*
(Bamidbar 30:3)

Many *Gedolim* explain: If a person is careful with what they say -- to not desecrate what goes out from their mouths; then Hashem will fulfill their blessings, etc. As the verse can be read, '*Like all that goes out of his mouth, **He** -- Hashem -- will do*'!

החלצו מאתכם אנשים לצבא
'Arm from with yourselves men for the legion'
(Bamidbar 31:3)

The **Sfas Emes** *zt"l* quotes a wonderful explanation on this: החלצו is also related to the word which means 'to remove'. Moshe Rabbeinu told *Bnei Yisroel* that they must '*remove from <u>themselves</u>*', meaning all self-interest in the matter; their intention in this war should not be for their own honor, and not for any human purpose -- but only for the glory of Heaven, as the *passuk* continues, '*to put the vengeance of Hashem in Midian.'*א

ובלעם בן בעור הרגו בחרב
'And Bilaam son of Bi'or they killed with the sword'
(Bamidbar 31:8)

Rashi *zt"l* brings the following from *Midrash Tanchuma*: Bilaam came against us and tried to exchange his craft for ours -- taking hold of the power of speech to try and curse us, and so too, we came upon him and utilized the craft of the nations -- the sword, like it says[58] '*And upon your sword you shall live*'.

---

[58] Bereishis 27:40.

We see clearly from this, says the **Chofetz Chaim** *zt"l*, that the craft-tool of a Jew is their power of speech. We can do incredible things with it, if we speak the way we are supposed to -- words of holiness, words of kindness, etc. And it is incumbent upon us to not degrade this incredible faculty of ours through forbidden speech, such as *lashon hara* and the like.[2]

❊ ❊ ❊ ❊ ❊ ❊ ❊ ❊ ❊ ❊ ❊ ❊ ❊

ויאמר אלעזר הכהן לאנשי הצבא. . . זאת חקת התורה

***'And Elazar the Kohen said to the men of the legion.
. . "This is the Decree of the Torah"'***

(Bamidbar 31:21)

Just like we asked back in *Parshas Chukas*, why זאת חקת התורה was said regarding the *Parah Adumah*, so too we ask here: Why was this language used here?

Sforno and **Chizkuni** *zt"l* say that this statement of Elazar's was referring back to what Moshe Rabbeinu had said in verse 19, about the men becoming purified from *tumas meis*, which is achieved through the ashes of the *Parah Adumah*, and therefore, these words are merely being used in reference to *Parah Adumah* again.

But in a different approach, **HaRav Moshe Feinstein** *zt"l* takes Elazar's statement to mean that what follows is *'the*

144

Decree of the Torah', and that is, the laws of *kashering* utensils.[59]

And from the language employed, says Rav Moshe, we infer that this thing -- the *kashering* of utensils, is a Decree that is a very all-encompassing one.[60] In what way is it? Explains Rav Moshe *zt"l*; from these laws, we see that it is possible to remove past impurity -- namely, in our lives, that of committing a transgression. And we learn from this that if, *Chas v'Shalom*, a person sins, or even if someone is, *Rachmana Litzlan*, saturated with sins -- they shouldn't despair. They have a possible fix; if they separate from their sins, and return in *Teshuva*, then they can be clean and pure, as if they didn't transgress!ª

ויאמר אלעזר הכהן אל אנשי הצבא. . . זאת חקת התורה אשר צוה השם את משה

***'And Elazar the Kohen said to the men of the legion.
. . "This is the Decree of the Torah, that Hashem
commanded Moshe'"***
(Bamidbar 31:21)

What follows the above *passuk* is the laws regarding *kashering* utensils, as noted above. **Rashi** *zt"l* brings from *Sifri Zuta* that we first must remove the rust from a vessel before we purge it -- which is called הגעלה.

---

[59] See v. 22-24.

[60] See Rav Moshe's commentary to 19:2.

So too, says the **Chofetz Chaim** *zt"l*, in spiritual matters: First, we must remove the "rust" of transgressions through *Teshuva*, including regret over our past misdeeds and resolutions for improvement in the future. After so, we must also correct ourselves in the area itself that we stumbled in. **כדרך תשמישו הגעלתו**, as *Rashi* brings on v. 23.[61]

❀ ❀ ❀ ❀ ❀ ❀ ❀ ❀ ❀ ❀ ❀ ❀ ❀ ❀

**ויאמרו אל משה עבדיך נשאו את ראש אנשי המלחמה
אשר בידנו ולא נפקד ממנו איש**

'And they [the leaders] said to Moshe; "Your servants have taken a count of the men of war who are in our hands, and not a man is missing from us."'
(Bamidbar 31:49)

Aside from the simple meaning, **Chazal** expound this phrase to mean that nobody was lost to a transgression.[62]

The **Ramban** *zt"l* expands on this: The whole time -- said the leaders -- the Midianim, including the women, were in our hands, and still, not one man left his fellow to go and transgress.

❀ ❀ ❀ ❀ ❀ ❀ ❀ ❀ ❀ ❀ ❀ ❀ ❀ ❀

---

[61] See verses 22-24 with *Rashi*.
[62] *Yevamos* 61a.

ויאמר משה לבני גד ולבני ראובן האחיכם יבאו
למלחמה ואתם תשבו פה. ולמה תניאון את לב בני
ישראל מעבר אל הארץ אשר נתן להם השם

*'And Moshe said to the children of Gad and to the
children of Reuven: "Shall your brothers come to
war, and you will stay here? And why do you
discourage the heart of the Children of Israel from
crossing to the Land that Hashem gave to them?"'*
(Bamidbar 32:6-7)

The Torah describes here how the people from the Tribes of Gad and Reuven had much livestock, and they saw the land <u>right outside</u> the Land of Israel, which was very good for animals. So they brought the question to Moshe Rabbeinu; could they have that land as an inheritance, instead of a portion inside of *Eretz Yisroel*? And Moshe Rabbeinu replies -- in the verses we quote -- that if they do so, they could cause others to not want to come across the *Yardein* (Jordan).[63]

Rashi *zt"l* explains that Moshe Rabbeinu was saying that they would potentially remove and hold back the hearts of the Jews from crossing over to Israel, because the People would be under the impression that the Tribes of Reuven and Gad are afraid of war and of the strength of the towns and people dwelling within the Land.

---

[63] Although, as things worked out, the Tribes of Gad and Reuven were allowed to take the portion they desired right outside of *Eretz Yisroel*. On condition, however, that they come over the Jordan and conquer the Land with the other Tribes. (See 32:16-32).

From this it is possible to see the great power of influence that every person holds. Moshe Rabbeinu was afraid that the children of Gad and Reuven could influence the rest of the *Bnei Yisroel* to not go into Israel -- even though they were, by far, the minority, in comparison to the rest of *Klal Yisroel*. And this goes for every one of us, as well. Even though we might be individuals, nevertheless, we must be extremely careful, because if we, *Chas v'Shalom*, give any bad example, it can, and very likely <u>will</u> have effect on others.

But it also goes the other way: If we can have such a negative effect on people if we act badly, *Chas v'Shalom*, then we also can influence so many people for good if we just make sure that we ourselves behave properly. By acting as we should, we can help the entire world!

People often like to tell others to do good. But perhaps just as -- or more -- important than that, is to <u>show</u> them to do good. As the colloquial expression goes, a picture is worth a thousand words.

וְהְיִיתֶם נְקִיִּם מֵהַשֵׁם וּמִיִשְׂרָאֵל
***'And you shall be clean (innocent) from Hashem and
from Israel'***
(Bamidbar 32:22)

We find a very interesting *Mishnah* in *Avos*:[64] 'Rebbe [Yehuda HaNasi] says: What is the upright path that a person should choose for himself? Whatever is a splendor to the one who does it, and [brings] to him splendor from people.'

At first glance, this *Mishnah* seems odd; are we trying to say that the main thing is finding favor in the eyes of people?

But in reality, we must realize that when we truly fulfill Hashem's Will, then others will also like/admire us. <u>Hashem</u> asks of us that we treat others properly! If we were careful to not lose our temper at people; if we were careful to always treat others with proper respect -- and this is all part of what Hashem wants from us -- then surely people would like us and be happy with our deeds as well! This is similar to what we are told in *Parshas Va'eschanan*,[65] '*And you shall guard and you shall do them [the Mitzvos], for it is your wisdom and understanding in the eyes of the peoples, who will hear all these decrees and they will say, "Only a wise and understanding people is this great nation!"*'

Keeping Hashem's dictates is first on the list, and it will actually bring along with it -- if kept in truth -- the admiration and like of others.[66]

---

[64] 2:1.

[65] Devarim 4:6.

[66] See below in <u>*Maasim Tovim*</u> on this verse.

**ויתן להם משה לבני גד ולבני ראובן ולחצי שבט מנשה
בן יוסף את ממלכת סיחן מלך האמרי ואת ממלכת עוג
מלך הבשן**

*'And Moshe gave to them -- to the children of Gad,
and to the children of Reuven, and to half the Tribe
of Menashe son of Yosef -- the [land of the] kingdom
of Sichon, king of the Emori, and the kingdom of Og,
king of the Bashan. . .'*
(Bamidbar 32:33)

Asks **HaRav Ben-Tzion Firer** *zt"l*; in all the give-and-take between Moshe Rabbeinu and the *Bnei Gad* and *Bnei Reuven*, the half-Tribe of Menashe is not mentioned once until after we are told that Moshe acceded to the request. Why were they not mentioned until now?

Suggests Rav Firer, Moshe Rabbeinu's plan was to get a portion from a Tribe to dwell on the other side of the Jordan with the Tribes of Reuven and Gad. Because he was hoping that the tribal unity of that Tribe -- *Shevet Menashe*, as it turned out, would propel the half across the Jordan to come to the aid of the other half, their tribal brothers, in the war to conquer *Eretz Yisroel*, and they would draw with them the *Bnei Gad* and *Bnei Reuven*.

To sum up, there was a possible concern that there might come to be a split between the Tribes, one more than just geographical. Moshe Rabbeinu wanted to prevent the border between *Eretz Yisroel* and outside of it from causing this possible separation, and he did what he could towards this end. The natural *achdus* of a Tribe -- in this case,

150

Menashe -- would unite both sides. And with this, we see why they weren't mentioned at first, when the request was made. They <u>weren't</u> part of that request, but were only brought in later.ⁿ

Another possible answer is given by the **Ramban** *zt"l*: At first, he says, the Tribe of Menashe didn't come to Moshe Rabbeinu about this. But when Moshe apportioned this area of land to the Tribes of Gad and Reuven, he saw that it was a bigger space than was fitting for them. So he asked who would like to take a share in it with them, and some men from the Tribe of Menashe wished to.

In a different vein, the *Avos D'Rabbi Nassan* teaches that the other side of the Jordan, where the Tribes of Reuven and Gad settled, was not a very spiritual place by nature.

Based on this, the **Netziv** *zt"l* suggests that really, it was Moshe Rabbeinu who wanted to put some of the Tribe of Menashe there with the other two Tribes, especially the family of Machir, since they had a lot of Torah scholars,[67] and they would light up the spiritual darkness of that area with the light of Torah.ᴵ

---

[67] See *Shoftim* 5:14.

❧Maasim Tovim❧

זאת חקת התורה. . . תעבירו באש
'This is the Decree of the Torah. . . you shall pass [them] through fire'
(Bamidbar 31:21,23)

There was a boy who would learn *Mishnayos* with his father every night, but he wasn't able to remember almost anything. The father was frustrated. He was hoping that his child would become a great *Talmid Chochom* (Torah scholar), and his son seemingly had a weak mind.

The father's concerns increased with the following episode: He was walking through the marketplace on Friday morning with his son, to buy fruits and vegetables for Shabbos. The son was looking around, spellbound by all the sights, listening to the vendors trying to outshout each other. One was yelling that he has the sweetest melons; another was shouting that he has the cheapest prices, and so on. That Shabbos afternoon, the father overheard his son chanting; "Get your sweetest melons here. . . We have the best prices. . ." The father realized that his son was able to repeat verbatim probably a hundred words he heard from the vendors. But he didn't understand: His son does have a good memory, so why can't he remember Torah? Could it be, *Chas v'Shalom*, that there's some blockage in his son's mind when it comes to holiness? Perhaps he is so attached to the things of This

World, that he can't understand anything spiritual? That thought frightened him, and he asked his *Rav* about it.

The *Rav* wisely explained, however: "You don't have to worry about your son. He has a good memory, and he can learn Torah as well. If you will learn *Mishnayos* with your son with the same passion and excitement as the merchants sell their wares, he will remember every word of the *Mishnayos*, as well."[1]

❧❧

והייתם נקיים מהשם ומישראל
***'And you shall be clean (innocent) from Hashem and
from Israel'***
(Bamidbar 32:22)

One time, one of the young married men from the **Chofetz Chaim** *zt"l*'s *yeshiva* asked him a *shaila*: He had been offered a Rabbinical position in a small city, and he wanted to know, how should he conduct himself with his congregation?

Answered the *Chofetz Chaim* with our verse, *'And you shall be clean (innocent) from Hashem and from Yisroel.'* First and foremost, the *Rav* needs to supervise to make sure that the Torah and *Mitzvos* are upheld -- he needs to worry about what Hashem wants -- which, of course, also includes that everyone is treated properly. And afterwards, he must worry about fulfilling his (other) duties towards the people.

If one tries to flip this order around -- trying to find favor in the eyes of people, and only afterwards, in the eyes of Hashem, then they won't be successful in either of them.ⁿ

✻✻✻✻✻✻✻✻✻✻✻✻

פרשת מסעי

Parshas Masei

אלה מסעי בני ישראל
'These are the travels of the Children of Israel'
(Bamidbar 33:1)

The Journeys of Klal Yisroel

The **Chida** *zt"l* brings an incredible thing on this *passuk*: The four Exiles (not including Egypt) are alluded to in the first letters of the words אלה מסעי בני

ישראל, as they are the same as those of אדום, *Edom*, מדי, *Maddai*, בבל, *Bavel*, and יון, *Yavan!*[א]

❧❧

HaRav Itzele of Volozhin *zt"l* teaches that every single person goes through, in some way -- whether physically, spiritually, or both -- the forty-two journeys, just like *Klal Yisroel* did, on an individual scale.[ב]

HaRav Binyomin Goldstein *shlit"a* elaborates beautifully on this concept, bringing a most wonderful parable which **Rashi** *zt"l* quotes from the *Midrash Tanchuma*:

"It can be likened to a king whose son became sick, so he took him to a far-away place to have him healed. On the way back, the father began to point out all the stages of their journey, saying to him, 'This is where we sat, here we were cold, here you had a headache, etc.'"

We must contemplate that we are each on our own individual journey, and the Torah itself is describing this exact journey. Ideally, we are all journeying to the right place: To the destination of righteousness and connection to Hashem *Yisbarach*. But we have many difficulties and challenges along the way. And, sometimes, we even veer off-course and have to bring ourselves back to the right path. But, after all is said and done, Hashem, our loving Father, lovingly points out all of the challenges and all of the difficulties that we endured in the "wilderness" of our lives, as if to say, "Look at how hard that was, and yet you kept going! Here you got a little sick; here you started to complain; but you made it. You really worked hard -- and I was there with you the entire time."

Rebbe Nachman of Breslov *zt"l* said, "This world is a narrow bridge; the main thing is not to be afraid." This means that we must have the courage to push forward and upward -- even if we don't feel like we're making much progress at all. We must constantly remember that Hashem, our Father, is with us every step along the way. The bridge of life may seem narrow, but we have no need to fear falling off, because Hashem is always here to guide us on the desired path. The holy writings teach us that to the extent that we yearn to reveal Hashem in our lives will we merit to perceive His Presence. The greatest comfort is to know that He is here the entire time.

HaRav Nissan Alpert *zt"l* explains another lesson of the journeys: There is much we can learn from the past. Especially our past actions and mistakes. We can glean insights into our nature, weaknesses, and what specific areas we need to work on. But unfortunately, not many people like to look back at nor think about their mistakes. We often prefer to dwell on our good actions. But this will ruin all the lessons and growth we could be getting from looking at and analyzing our past errors!

156

Therefore, Hashem told Moshe Rabbeinu to record the names of all forty-two journeys, which were not mere place-names, but allusions to the occurrences that took place there, and the mistakes we had made, so that we should not forget them, but rather make sure to learn from them.¹

אלה מסעי בני ישראל
'These are the travels of the Children of Israel'
(Bamidbar 33:1)

Chazal say (*Midrash Rabbah; Tanchuma*); why did these places merit being written in the Torah? Because they accepted *Klal Yisroel* in the *Midbar* (Wilderness) as their guests. And in the future, HaKadosh Baruch Hu is going to give a reward to the *Midbar* -- for, right now it is a dry, desolate place, but He is going to transform it into an inhabited land, with lots of water and trees.

From here, says the *Midrash*, a person should derive a tremendous lesson for themselves: If the Wilderness, which doesn't have any knowledge nor mind of its own will be given such reward, how much more so we human beings, that if we host a *talmid chochom* in our house, and give him from our own things, what incredible reward we will surely get!

HaRav Eliyahu Chaim Cohen *shlit"a* expands on this *Midrash*: The *Midbar*, as we know, obviously did not have any prior intention to host *Klal Yisroel*, and it could not have resisted either! It is an inanimate *Midbar*! And nevertheless, since it still benefited *Klal Yisroel*, Hashem will not hold back any reward from it, and He publicizes the names of the places where we stayed. How very much more so if we benefit another human being by <u>our own choice</u>, with the intention to do so, and <u>with</u> good will, Hashem will certainly reward us many times over![7]

ואלה מסעיהם למוצאיהם

'And these were their journeys according to their departures.'
(Bamidbar 33:2)

Says the **Abarbanel** *zt"l*, the journeys that *Klal Yisroel* took in the *Midbar* allude to the future Redemption (may it be soon, and in our days!), as the *Navi* Micha prophecies from Hashem, *'Like the days of your going out from the land of Egypt, I will show him wonders.'*[68] Meaning that just like when we left Egypt, Hashem led us in the *Midbar* through these forty-two journeys, so too in the time of the Redemption, He will lead us once again through them, as it says in *Sefer Yechezkel*, that Hashem will bring us to the *'Wilderness of the nations.'*[69]

It could be, says the *Abarbanel*, that this is what is hinted to in our *passuk*: *'These are their journeys according to their*

---

[68] *Micha* 7:16

[69] *Yechezkel* 20:35

departures' -- meaning, that we will again pass through these places when we depart from the last Exile!

✻ ✻ ✻ ✻ ✻ ✻ ✻ ✻ ✻ ✻ ✻ ✻ ✻ ✻

ולא תקחו כפר לנפש רצח אשר הוא רשע למות
'You shall not accept ransom for the life of a murderer who is guilty of death'
(Bamidbar 35:31)

Says **HaRav Moshe Shternbuch** *shlit"a*: This *passuk* comes to teach that someone who has committed a transgression should not imagine that they can save themselves from punishment through "a redemption" or "ransom", of giving a lot of charity, for example. Only through true *teshuva* can one merit forgiveness and atonement.

And Rav Shternbuch elaborates: We must remember that a *Mitzvah* cannot cover up a sin. If, *Chas v'Shalom*, we have done something wrong, doing a *Mitzvah* will not get rid of that sin. Of course, we should certainly be trying to turn around and actively pursue and perform *Mitzvos*, but the only thing that will purify us from our transgression(s) is *teshuva*. Hashem does not accept "bribes" -- in any fashion.ה

✻ ✻ ✻ ✻ ✻ ✻ ✻ ✻ ✻ ✻ ✻ ✻ ✻ ✻

וישב בה עד מות הכהן הגדול
'And he shall dwell in it until the death of the Kohen Gadol'

(Bamidbar 35:25)

The question is; why is this specifically the thing which enables the accidental-killer to "go free" from the *Arei Miklat* (cities of refuge)?

As we know, this accidental-killer, although their act was completely unintentional, still, the relative of the person who was killed -- the *go'eil hadam* -- would be very upset at them and would perhaps attempt to avenge their deceased relative, which would actually be permitted, in this case. However, in the *Arei Miklat*, they were safe from this possibility.

Now, explains the **Rambam** *zt"l*, it is the nature of a human being that if, *Chas v'Shalom*, a tragedy befalls them, and then afterwards, a tragedy befalls others, which is just as severe or more so, that they don't feel quite as alone in their suffering, and in some odd way, it kind of consoles them a little. The relatives of the person who was accidentally slain will most likely be quite upset at the accidental-killer, and the desire for revenge will stay with them for a while. However, when the *Kohen Gadol* -- who is just about the most beloved of people to everyone -- passes away, it is a national event of mourning, and this will quiet the anger and passion of the *go'eil hadam*, to a certain extent, as perhaps they won't feel quite as alone in their suffering anymore. Thus, it is now safe for the accidental-killer to emerge from his exile in the *Arei Miklat*.[1]

'

The **Abarbanel** *zt"l* suggests that the death of the *Kohen Gadol* is an event that shakes everybody up, and arouses people to *teshuva*. Therefore, there is reason to believe that also the *go'eil hadam* will introspect a lot, and conquer their desire for revenge. This will take away the threat from the accidental-killer.ᵀ

In a very different take, **HaRav Yaakov Tzvi Mecklenburg** *zt"l* explains that among accidental-killers who would be sent to the *Arei Miklat*, there are varying levels of culpability, depending, for example, on their level of negligence in the deed. And only Hashem can know these details and "sentence" each person for the time there that they personally deserve. For this reason, an accidental-killer's ability to leave the city of refuge is made dependent on the death of the *Kohen Gadol* -- something which only Hashem can control. And He, in His perfect system of Justice, will make sure that each person stays in exile for exactly as long as they should.ⁿ

ויסעו מרפידים ויחנו במדבר סיני. ויסעו ממדבר סיני
ויחנו בקברות התאוה.

'And they journeyed from Rephidim and they encamped in the Wilderness of Sinai. And they

journeyed from the Wilderness of Sinai and they encamped in Kivros HaTaavah.'
(Bamidbar 33:15-16)

Rephidim, *Mechilta* tells us, is the place where the Jews 'loosened their hands from the Torah' (we were given some laws before coming to Sinai).

However, **Rashi zt"l** quotes[70] from *Mechilta* that just as our coming to the Wilderness of Sinai was with *Teshuva*, so too our traveling from *Rephidim* was with *Teshuva*.

Based upon this, we may derive a lesson from the above verses: With *Teshuva*, a person can go from a state of deterioration (as the Jews were in *Rephidim*) to being on such a great level, as we were at Sinai.

But, the flip side is also true: We can never grow complacent, because, if a person is not careful, they can go from a very high level -- Sinai -- and fall to a level of *Kivros HaTaavah, Chas v'Shalom.* We must always be vigilant and on watch for the *yetzer hara*'s traps.

צו את בני ישראל ונתנו ללוים מנחלת אחזתם ערים לשבת

'Command the Children of Israel, and they shall give to the Leviim from the inheritance of their heritage cities in which to dwell'

---

[70] Shemos 19:2

(Bamidbar 35:2)

Asks **HaRav Zalman Sorotzkin** *zt"l*; it is very understandable that Hashem did not designate a portion of the Land to the Leviim, so as to not burden or distract them from their special Service in the *Mishkan*. However, why did He not command, as part of the apportionment of the Land, that houses be allotted to them, but instead made it that the *Bnei Yisroel* would give it to them as some sort of a gift?

Rav Sorotzkin suggests two answers: #1, It was in order to show supporters of Torah for all generations that they cannot just "fulfill their obligation" with giving *maaser*, or helping with expenses for food. We must also concern ourselves <u>personally</u> with making sure that those who learn Torah have a roof over their heads, and a house to live in.

And #2, as we know, the Leviim were given houses in and were to settle in the *Arei Miklat*. Now, if someone unintentionally killed a person (see above), and had to flee to one of these cities, they might feel like a stranger and outsider, who depends on the kindness of those who live there to accept them. Therefore, Hashem wanted the *Bnei Yisroel* to even give the houses as a gift to the Leviim, so that anyone who needed to flee there would feel comfortable, knowing that they also have a portion in these cities, as the *Bnei Yisroel* gave them to the Leviim on the very condition that they would be open, available, and shared with anyone who might end up needing to stay there.^ע

❁❁❁❁❁❁❁❁❁❁❁❁❁❁

Maasim Tovim

ויחנו במדבר סיני

'And they encamped in the wilderness of Sinai.'

(Bamidbar 33:15)

HaRav Yisroel Salanter *zt"l* was a tremendous *baal mussar,* and made time to speak to and help others. But he also had a rigorous learning schedule, studying Torah for 16-18 hours a day!

Rav Yisroel kept this up even in his old age, and someone once asked him why, seeing as though by this time he probably knew just about "everything"!

[Obviously, the main reason why Rav Yisroel learned was to fulfill Hashem's Will], but he replied powerfully, "So that the tailor's son in Paris should not become an apostate." He was highlighting the incredible effects that Torah study has, on other people, as well, and even those who are in a far-away place from where you are studying!'

זאת תהיה לכם הארץ לגבלתיה סביב

'This shall be for you the Land, according to its borders, all around.'

(Bamidbar 34:12)

The *mashgiach*, **HaRav Mordechai Finkelman** *shlit"a* relates about his *Rebbe*, **HaRav Moshe Wolfson** *shlit"a*, how intense of a love he has for *Eretz Yisroel*, and he told over one such example of that love in an incident that occurred several years ago:

When Rav Finkelman was much younger, he once went to *Eretz Yisroel* with Rav Wolfson *shlit"a* for *Lag BaOmer*. They stayed in Yerushalayim for Shabbos, and there were a lot of amazing *Yerushalmi Rabbonim* who gave *drashos* where they were. In short, the Shabbos was a most uplifting one.

On *Motzaei Shabbos*, when the busses came to take them to Meron, where the gravesite of Rabbi Shimon bar Yochai *zt"l* is located, Rav Finkelman remarked to Rav Wolfson, "The *Rebbe* should know that I could go home right now. Shabbos was so uplifting, that for it alone the entire ticket here was worth it."

Rav Wolfson looked somewhat disappointed, and said back to him, "When I first walked off the plane, and my feet touched the holy soil of *Eretz Yisroel*, the entire trip would have been worth it. I could have gone home right then."

❈ ❈ ❈ ❈ ❈ ❈ ❈ ❈ ❈ ❈ ❈ ❈ ❈ ❈

Chazak Chazak V'Nischazeik!

May Hashem help us all – and the entire Klal Yisroel -- to take everything we learned in Sefer Bamidbar with us always, and to enter with a holy enthusiasm to Sefer Devarim!

Sources:

Bamidbar

א Tiferes Shimshon

ב Daas Torah

ג Emes L'Yaakov

ד Oznayim LaTorah

ה Chofetz Chaim al HaTorah

ו Darash Moshe

Nasso

א Peninim on the Torah, sixteenth series, with permission from the author, HaRav Avraham Leib Scheinbaum shlit"a

ב Taama D'Krah

ג Chofetz Chaim al HaTorah

ד Emes L'Yaakov

ה Chofetz Chaim al HaTorah

ו Ateres HaMikra

ז Maayanah shel Torah; Pe'er Publishing

ח Heard from the Mashgiach, HaRav Mordechai Finkelman shlit"a

ט Heard from my father and Rebbe, HaRav T. S. Chesler shlit"a, who saw it in the sefer The Baal Shem of Michelstadt; Feldheim Publishers

Behaaloscha

א Sfas Emes 5635

ב HaLekach Vi'HaLibuv

ג Maayanah shel Torah; Pe'er Publishing

ד Shemen HaTov

ה Tiferes Shimshon

ו Heard from my Rebbe, HaRav Moshe Shulman shlit"a

ז Simchas Yosef

ח Heard from my Rebbe, HaRav Avraham Kaplan shlit"a

ט HaMeoros HaGedolim

י Ksav Sofer al HaTorah

יא Nachalas Tzvi

יב Taam v'Daas Shemos 16:7

יג Heard from the Mashgiach, HaRav Mordechai Finkelman shlit"a

יד Reproduced from A Gadol in Our Time: Stories about Rav Chaim Kanievsky, with permission of the copyright holders, ArtScroll / Mesorah Publications, Ltd.

טו HaMeoros HaGedolim

Shelach

א Heard from the Mashgiach, HaRav Mordechai Finkelman shlit"a

ב Meshech Chochmah

ג Brought in Torah L'Daas

ד Aish Kodesh

ה Avodas Yisroel

ו Zechor l'Miriam, in Divrei Eliyahu

ז Shabbos Gems

Korach

א Lechem Yehuda

ב Noam Elimelech; end of Likutei Shoshanah

ג Ner Yisroel; told to me by my Rebbe, HaRav Moshe Shulman shlit"a

ד Meshech Chochmah

ה Toras Avigdor

ו Darash Moshe

ז B'Derech Eitz HaChaim, vol. 1; quoted in Growth Through Torah; Bnei Yaakov Publications

ח Shabbos Gems

Chukas

א Darash Moshe

ב Apiryon

ג Adapted from Magen Avraham, as explained by my Rebbe, HaRav Moshe Shulman shlit"a

ד Chofetz Chaim al HaTorah

ה Kovetz Igros, vol. 1

ו Nikolsburg.org

ז Avodas Yisroel; and heard from my Rebbe, HaRav Moshe Shulman shlit"a

ח Reproduced from Maayan Beis HaShoeivah, by HaRav Shimon Schwab zt"l, with permission of the copyright holders, ArtScroll / Mesorah Publications, Ltd.

ט Avodas Yisroel, and heard from my Rebbe, HaRav Moshe Shulman shlit"a

י Darash Moshe

יא Shabbos Gems

יב Meshech Chochmah

יג Chofetz Chaim al HaTorah

יד Heard from my Rebbe, HaRav Moshe Shulman shlit"a

טו Related to me by Rebbetzin Rosenblatt shetichyeh

Balak

א Sparks of Torah, with permission from the author, HaRav Dovid Nussbaum shlit"a

ב Apiryon

ג Darash Moshe

ד Vezos HaBracha quoted in Peninim on the Torah; sixteenth series, with permission from the author

ה Darash Moshe

ו Emes L'Yaakov

ז Kol Eliyahu

ח Chofetz Chaim al HaTorah

ט She'eiris Menachem, as explained in Yagdil Torah

י Reproduced from Four Chassidic Masters, by HaRav Avraham J. Twerski zt"l, (Shaar Press), with permission of the copyright holders, ArtScroll / Mesorah Publications, Ltd.

יא Heard from HaRav Shmuel Greenberg shlit"a

יב HaMeoros HaGedolim

Pinchas

א Maayanah Shel Torah; Pe'er Publishing

ב Biurei HaDaf; Sanhedrin

ג Nesivos Shalom

ד Derech Chaim Tochachas Mussar, in Shnei Luchos HaBris Vol. 3

ה Chofetz Chaim al HaTorah

ו The Pleasant Way, by HaRav Sholom Smith shlit"a; Israel Bookshop Publications

ז Meshech Chochmah

ח Madreigas HaAdam, Tikkun HaMiddos, as cited in HaMeoros HaGedolim

ט HaEimek Davar

י Darash Moshe

יא Heard from my Rebbe, HaRav Moshe Shulman shlit"a

יב Heard from my Rebbe, HaRav Avraham Kaplan shlit"a

Mattos

א Sfas Emes in the name of Meforshim; as quoted in Maayanah Shel Torah; Pe'er Publishing

ב Chofetz Chaim al HaTorah

ג Darash Moshe

ד Chofetz Chaim al HaTorah

ה Hegyonah shel Torah

ו HaEimek Davar to Devarim 3:16

ז Torah Wellsprings

ח Maasei LaMelech in Chofetz Chaim al HaTorah

Masei

א Nachal Kedomim

ב Heard from my Rebbe, HaRav Shalom Kelemer shlit"a

ג Limudei Nissan

ד Otzros HaTorah

ה Taam v'Daas

ו Moreh Nevuchim 3:40

ז As explained in Maayanah shel Torah; Pe'er Publishing

ח HaKsav v'HaKabbalah

ט Oznayim laTorah

י Related by HaRav Shmuel Greenberg shlit"a